Worst in the World

International Football
at the Bottom of
the FIFA Rankings

Aidan Williams

**BENNION
KEARNY**

Published by Bennion Kearny Limited
6 Woodside
Churnet View Road
Oakamoor
ST10 3AE

www.BennionKearny.com

For Sarah, Elliot and Iris

Aidan Williams

Aidan Williams hails from Newcastle upon Tyne, is the Editor of *The Sports Book Review* and has written for various football websites including *These Football Times, Back Page Football, Sports Haze, UFWC* and *The Worst in the World*. He also writes various travel articles to balance out the sporting obsession.

Having lived in Japan, and spent other extended periods abroad, Aidan has developed something of a global perspective to his sporting interests - something that is reflected in the themes of his writing, more of which can be found at *aidanwilliamswriter.wordpress.com*

* * * * *

My thanks go to James at Bennion Kearny for giving me this opportunity and for all his hard work in editing everything I sent him, and to his colleague Adam for first asking me if I would like to write a book.

My research has been aided by a host of invaluable web resources, books, and newspaper articles – some very obscure, some less so. All have proved useful in building a picture of the events, teams and participants in some of the lesser-known activities of world football.

To the small island of Montserrat for triggering my memory of their Other Final while I hovered over it in a helicopter, and sparking the idea of the *Worst in the World*.

And finally to Sarah for reading the initial drafts and providing early feedback, for encouraging me throughout, and never doubting that I could do it.

Table of Contents

Introduction

The rain continued to pour down from the dark night sky as it had done all evening, but neither the players in blue, nor their small band of disbelieving supporters seemed to care. In the small, sparsely populated stands, the few witnesses to this historic moment hailed their unlikely heroes, while the devastated visiting supporters, equally disbelieving, vented their anger on their own team. The referee had blown the full time whistle only moments earlier, prompting the San Marino national team players to launch into a wild celebration befitting winning the World Cup or European Championship in one of Europe's grandest stadiums. And yet they hadn't achieved anything remotely near that level of success. They were celebrating nothing more than a goalless draw on a dark, dank and sodden November evening in 2014 in their tiny national stadium.

But they had also achieved something significant. They had avoided defeat for only the fifth time in their 123-match history. After six-and-a-half long years, and 39 matches as being officially the joint worst national team in world football, San Marino had finally climbed off the bottom of FIFA's world rankings. The monkey was off their back, for the time being at least.

Quite why avoiding defeat was such an unlikely and unusual occurrence for San Marino can be easily explained by a look at their population statistics. As of 2013, the official population of San Marino was a shade over 31,000 in a country of just over 60km^2; the very definition of a microstate. To put that in context, San Marino's entire population could fit into Wembley Stadium almost three times over.

San Marino's relative handful of residents is something they share in common with many of the other nations to have found themselves stuck at the bottom of FIFA's world rankings, cut adrift from the rest of the footballing world with the unwanted label of being the worst national teams on the planet. Now it was San Marino's turn to bid farewell to their membership of that exclusive club and climb the rankings… all thanks to that improbable goalless draw.

* * * * *

1

FIFA's world rankings are a veritable minefield of complication, confusion and apparent conjecture at times but their intention is to allow a direct comparison of the relative strengths of national teams across the globe. They are increasingly used to decide seeding pots for both qualifying and finals tournaments and so carry a little more significance than most feel is worthy, given the numerous inconsistencies they seem to throw up. Such worries about tournament seeding are far from the minds of those at the bottom of the rankings, however.

As with any sport, football is naturally obsessed with discovering who the best is. Leagues and cups are designed, of course, with this simple premise in mind: a meritocracy where the cream rises to the top to be acclaimed by all and sundry. International football has a vast array of competitions to decide who the best team is, at any given time, in a number of varied geographical clusters. The World Cup, European Championship, Copa America, and so on, all crown their champions every few years. Winners are also crowned in a succession of smaller areas, such as the East Asian Championship, Caribbean Cup and – once upon a time – the British Home Championship.

While, in some cases, it is clear who the worst team in any given tournament is, as they suffer one humbling defeat after another, it is less clear to determine who is the worst of them all. FIFA, in their infinite wisdom, came up with a means of doing this in the early 1990s. Or to be more accurate, they came up with a way of calculating who the best was, and exactly where everyone else sat behind them. And so the FIFA World Rankings were born; an attempt at identifying the state of play that has caused much ridicule and criticism ever since.

And while FIFA weren't intentionally trying to highlight the worst national team in the world, the rankings did bestow that ignominious title on one, or frequently more than one, country at a time. It is, of course, impossible to know for sure which of several nations - who are unlikely to ever face each other - happens to be the worst. This is where the rankings fall down. Is a European micro-nation, who only ever faces other European teams of considerably greater populations and resources than itself, a worse team than a Caribbean nation who only plays once every four years and loses to a neighbouring speck in the ocean? Nobody can say for sure, but without the possibility of such nations regularly facing each other, the rankings are the best means available.

FIFA rankings have frequently come in for criticism largely because they often seem to bear little resemblance to reality. This is a symptom of the fact that several years' worth of results are taken into account. The calculations used have gone through a few tweaks to a greater or lesser extent over the years, but the crux is the same. Wins garner more points than draws, and wins in competitive matches garner more than those in friendlies; tournament finals warrant an increasingly greater number of potential points as teams progress to the latter stages. The strength of a team's regional confederation has a bearing, as does the strength of the opposition. Currently, defeats gain no points no matter whom they were against, though at one time that wasn't the case. It's a complicated business and one that nobody can seemingly agree on.

At present, four years' worth of results are taken into account, with points gained carrying exponentially less weight as they become older before being expunged altogether once that time limit is reached. The upshot of this is that a team's points can change – month to month – even if they don't play. For a long time, eight years of results were taken into account, and this meant that a successful tournament some years earlier left many a team artificially high in spite of poor recent results. For example, Greece climbed the rankings after their victory in Euro 2004 and those points kept them high in the rankings for a long time in spite of repeated insipid results in the years after.

Conversely, a team that doesn't have to qualify for a tournament, an upcoming World Cup host for instance, will only play friendly matches for a two year period and consequently tumble down the rankings as those friendly matches don't bring in as many ranking points as the teams winning competitive qualifying matches. Brazil dropped as low as 18th at one point in the lead up to the 2014 World Cup they hosted. A flaw in the system no doubt.

Because of these anomalies, some alternative ranking methods have sprung up, notably the ELO system which uses a modified version of a calculation used for chess rankings. Many argue that the ELO rankings provide a truer picture of a team's relative performance levels than the FIFA rankings, and that may be the case when looking at the teams higher up. But when looking at the bottom of the ELO table there are teams who rarely play at all, such as Kiribati, Palau, or the Vatican. Also listed are many other non-FIFA affiliated countries such as Greenland, Northern Cyprus, Wallis & Futuna and Monaco among many others. Since these nations don't play "official" internationals, or play so infrequently as to be a near-irrelevance, it seems best to discard the ELO system as a means of identifying the worst national team in the world and focus solely on the FIFA rankings. Although some of the teams in the nether regions of those rankings play infrequently too, they do at least belong to FIFA and one of its regional confederations and so take part in tournaments rather more frequently than the non-FIFA national teams do.

* * * * *

San Marino, like the other nations to have been stranded at the bottom of the world rankings at some point in their history, have suffered the distinction of being regarded as the official worst national team in the world; a baton of ignominy passed from one small outlying nation to another. Or more often, it has been held jointly by a cluster of the weak for sometimes years on end. This book aims to look at the exploits and dramas of the worst national teams in the world as they strive to climb away from the foot of the rankings.

There are teams that are utterly out of their depth and have suffered heavy and humiliating defeats, occasionally on a record-breaking scale. Teams that have found success by bringing in outside expertise or by exploiting FIFA's rules on international eligibility, and those who have found a modicum of success by sticking to their own. There is the occasional, relative, giant killing, and more than a few countries finding themselves stuck at the bottom for extended periods of time.

The profile of the worst football nations reached its zenith when, in 2002, an enterprising Dutchman organised an alternative World Cup Final, played on the same day as the real final in Japan, between the two teams ranked at the foot of FIFA's list at the time: Bhutan and Montserrat. That match, and its accompanying film, provided the inspiration for this endeavour following the fortunes, or lack thereof, of the worst national teams in the world.

4

The fate of sporting underdogs has long stirred the passions of many a follower, possibly because there is something pleasing about seeing apparently 'ordinary' people - waiters, schoolteachers, bricklayers, or in the case of San Marino's goalkeeper, an accountant - taking on the elite of the sport. As described by James Montague in his homage to the marathon of World Cup qualification, *Thirty-One Nil*, the true outsider provides a degree of fascination to those spectating. "The world of professional sport can only be viewed longingly from the stands by most people. But the outsider? He is one of us, moulded in our image, recognisable to the touch."

If those players in the worst teams in the world are perhaps not quite "one of us", they are at least not so far removed from those watching as is the case with most professional sports people. The elite are viewed as just that: the elite. Whereas the outsider, the underdog, the hapless minnow – we can empathise with them in their struggles, in their limitations, and in their usual sporting demise. Perhaps too there is some degree of morbid fascination, at times, in seeing a poor team really taken apart.

In looking at the wrong end of the table, so to speak, my aim is to bring some attention to those nations whose football aspirations lie not in trophies or even qualification, but simply in the love of the game and the pride of representing their country.

Chapter 1: Out of their Depth

By this point, the American Samoan team were beyond even humiliation. The bedraggled and deflated group stood in a line, their baggy shirts flapping in the light evening breeze. With arms around each other's shoulders they faced the appreciative Australian crowd and sang, in spite of the tears welling up in many of the players' eyes. It was a song of pride, of defiance, of home. But home must have felt a long way off for the youthful squad who had just become world news, and not in a good way.

'After the game we walked into the locker room, I bowed my head down and I cried a little bit,' the goalkeeper Nicky Salapu recalled years later in an interview with the *Born Offside* website. 'I felt very embarrassed and like I don't want to play soccer anymore.'[1]

Listed by FIFA as the worst team in the world at the time of their World Cup qualifying match with Australia in April 2001, American Samoa had overcome a seemingly endless string of obstacles to even get that far, not least their own lack of experience at the rarefied level of international football. They were startled rabbits in the bright Australian headlights, painfully aware of what was about to hit them but unable to conjure up any way of avoiding it. If the sporting obstacles in their way weren't enough of a test, one or two administrative banana skins placed in their path enhanced the difficulty of the challenge.

An unincorporated territory of the United States of America in the South Pacific Ocean, American Samoa is made up of five main islands and a handful of atolls, and has a population of a shade over 55,000 for whom football sits some way behind American Football and Basketball in the list of sporting priorities. They became members of FIFA in 1998 as part of the governing body's extensive membership increase of that era. Along with the likes of other non-independent nations, or more accurately territories, such as Guam, Montserrat and the Turks and Caicos Islands, American Samoa took their place at world football's table; the beneficiaries of an expansionist and global football development policy.

In their years as an 'unofficial' football nation, they had achieved the dubious feat of only ever winning one match and losing the remaining nine, many of them by a hefty margin. Their lone unofficial victory actually came in their very first international match at the 1983 South Pacific Games in neighbouring Western Samoa, with a 3-0 win over the equally unofficial national team of the French territory of Wallis and Futuna. What came next, however, would set the tone for years to come.

The occasional narrow defeat would inevitably be followed, sooner or later, by a defeat of more epic proportions, as even up against weak opposition they proved themselves to be way out of their depth time and time again. The 1987 South Pacific Games was a particular low point, with New Caledonia putting ten goals past the American Samoans, only to be superseded by Papua New Guinea who scored twenty without reply. That was enough to send American Samoa into footballing hibernation for a few years before returning for the 1994 Polynesian Cup. Although beaten there three times out of three, they were mercifully spared a thrashing and, in fact, only once lost by more than a single goal. Such was the backdrop of regular defeat against which FIFA membership was secured.

Becoming an official football nation did little to improve their fortunes. By the time the World Cup qualifiers came around in 2001, their first tentative stab at the biggest tournament of them all, American Samoa had played eight more Polynesian Cup matches as a fully-fledged member of the FIFA family and lost them all. Tahiti inflicted the most damage with 12-0 and 18-0 victories.

The 2002 edition of the World Cup, the finals of which would take place in Japan and South Korea, was the first that American Samoa were eligible to take part in. The Oceania confederation had grown relatively quickly in the late twentieth century from what previously amounted to little more than a playoff between Australia and New Zealand into a regional qualification process involving ten teams. The Oceania Football Confederation (OFC) plumped for a slightly misguided qualifying process that would split the ten teams into two groups of five, thus pitting the smallest of minnows against a country the size of a continent without any preliminary round to weed out the weakest of the weak. American Samoa, along with their neighbours Samoa, Tonga and Fiji were put in a group with the relative might of Australia.

The Socceroos of Australia had narrowly missed out on the 1998 World Cup Finals, contriving to throw qualification away by conceding two late goals to Iran when a place in the finals was all but assured. The scars from that trauma still ran deep when the subsequent tournament came around and Australia were determined to open their 2002 World Cup campaign in a professional and ruthless manner. Sterner tests would surely await them further down the line, but the opening group was a chance to exorcise a few demons ahead of more crucial matches later on.

Thankfully, for their opposition, the Australian squad was missing many of its top stars plying their trade in some of Europe's stronger leagues. A combination of the tournament occurring during the crucial last weeks of the European season, and a lack of any real need to drag their star men all the way to Australia for what was always likely to be something of a walk in the park for the Australians, made them surplus to requirements. Furthermore, FIFA, under pressure from the clubs of some of the European-based players, requested that the Australian coach Frank Farina not select any of the higher profile names for this tournament. Those players, they argued, simply wouldn't be needed in this initial qualifying group, and it was pointless antagonising their clubs for such a formality. In the end several of the highest profile players weren't called up, but the Australian squad still featured the likes of John Aloisi of Coventry City, Hayden Foxe of West Ham United and Craig Moore and Tony Vidmar of Glasgow Rangers. The bigger names of Harry Kewell, Mark Schwarzer, Mark Viduka and Brett Emerton, among others, all remained at their clubs, not needed for this anticipated straightforward opening to the Socceroos' World Cup campaign.

To add to the difficulties on a sporting level for the American Samoans and their fellow minnows, this group would be hosted by Australia. Naturally, they were the most practical host given the facilities and resources of their opponents, but it did stack the odds even more in Goliath's favour. Likewise, the other opening round group of OFC qualification was hosted by the other rich and more successful nation, New Zealand – if not a Goliath themselves, then at least Goliath's little brother.

Australia selected the coastal city of Coffs Harbour to host the group; a scenic conurbation in northern New South Wales on the

Pacific Highway to the Gold Coast, with numerous beaches and marinas against the backdrop of the Great Dividing Range behind. As if to emphasise the scale of the task ahead of the visiting American Samoans, the population of Coffs Harbour was not much less than that of their homeland.

A squad of twenty was selected to represent the worst team in world football as it made its maiden bow in the World Cup. A squad containing a mix of the best and most experienced players the islands had to offer along with a smattering of youth, unscarred by past failures. Making use of FIFA's 'grandparents clause' with the approval of the OFC, the team selection contained several players originally hailing from neighbouring Samoa, formerly Western Samoa, but whose heritage or indeed current residency was American Samoan. This is a rule that is increasingly exploited in international football, and not only by the weaker nations seeking to bolster their talent pool. The likes of the Republic of Ireland made great use of the 'Granny Rule' to lure many a player from England and Scotland to represent them over the years, as have the United States more recently. In addition, there was the use of residency rules to add a few players not of American Samoan descent but who currently resided there to play for the national team. Again, this is a widespread tactic in modern football times used by many a national team – think Diego Costa for Spain, Eduardo for Croatia, Marcel Desailly and Patrick Vieira for France and so on.

But then came the hammer blow, inflicted by FIFA. An eleventh hour intervention from football's governing body ruled those players not holding a US passport, as fully-fledged American Samoans do, would be ineligible to play. Instantly nineteen of the twenty-man squad were excluded, with only the twenty-year-old goalkeeper Nicky Salapu carrying the required document. Just how does an already weak national team squad recover from such a setback on the eve of a World Cup qualifying tournament? With great difficulty.

Plans by the head coach, Tunoa Lui, to use players from the national under-20 squad were also scuppered because the majority of them were sitting their high school exams at the time. Not a problem that is typically encountered by national teams higher up the food chain! Has a World Cup campaign ever got off to such an inauspicious start, and before a ball had even been kicked? Withdrawing might have been the sensible thing to do at this point. The trip surely couldn't be salvaged now with only likely humiliation awaiting. But, instead, American Samoa blindly stumbled on, with significant encouragement from the OFC not to withdraw.

A replacement squad was flown out post-haste comprising of US passport holders from the youth squad, mostly in their teenage years, with three of them only fifteen years old. This patchwork national team produced a sixteen 'man' squad with an average age of just nineteen. One player went by the highly appropriate name of Baby Mulipola. This team of teenagers joined the only player of any experience worth speaking of and the last man standing from the original squad, the aforementioned goalkeeper Nicky Salapu.

To make matter worse, many of the youth squad arrived without any boots and subsequently two of them succumbed to injury during their opening 13-0 defeat to Fiji. This rather disastrous debut in the tournament, and indeed in World Cup football, went awry after a mere three minutes with Fiji taking the lead through a penalty. Thankfully the Fijians eased off somewhat having led by eight goals at half time, but any remaining shred of American Samoan optimism, if there could possibly have been any by this point in proceedings, was well and truly shattered. They had at least avoided a repeat of their, at the time, record defeat, the previously mentioned 18-0 loss to Tahiti a couple of years earlier.

Things didn't go much better in American Samoa's second outing, losing 8-0 to neighbours Samoa, but it is what had happened immediately prior to that match which would be most worrying for the youthful islanders.

Australia faced Tonga in their opening match of the group a couple of hours before the clash of the two Samoas. The Socceroos stormed their way into the record books with a 22-0 win; a new world record victory in international football, ahead of Kuwait's 20-0 thrashing of another severely outclassed lowly ranked nation, Bhutan, in an Asian Cup qualifier just a year before. Naturally, therefore, it was also a World Cup record, beating the previous 'best' of Iran's 19-0 win over Guam only six months earlier. John Aloisi, of then Premier League Coventry City, grabbed six of the twenty-two goals in Australia's record-breaking victory in what his coach, Frank Farina, found to be a rather meaningless challenge. 'Oceania have to look seriously at the format,' he said, with ominous portends for their upcoming opponents. 'It was embarrassing. No one was a winner. We had nothing to gain from it and neither did they.'[2] It does beg the question as to why, if they had nothing to gain, other than the three points for their victory of course, Australia felt the need to push on to such an extent as to score twenty-two times.

Australia's record win was greeted with much guffawing delight by the world's observers, relishing the Socceroos' record-breaking exploits. There would be no guffaws from the American Samoans however. They were up next. The unrelenting Australian behemoth was almost upon them. The worst team in the world, ranked 203rd and last in FIFA's rankings would be up against a team ranked 75th with a population more than four hundred times their own, and would of course be playing with a de facto youth squad. In the face of such apparently insurmountable odds, American Samoa coach Tunoa Lui revealed how his deeply religious team sought assistance: 'We are here to learn. We have had a lot of problems but we don't give up,' he stated defiantly. A little more desperately, he added, 'We are asking the Lord to help keep the score down,'[3] The Lord would have his work cut out.

Match day arrived and the crowd in the Coffs Harbour International Stadium, a relatively sparse one on a warm autumnal weekday evening, were sat either in the small main stand alongside the touchline, or on grass banks circling the ends of the oval stadium. As settings for record-breaking football exploits go, it was a fairly nondescript one. The stadium, little more than a field with a tiny grandstand surrounded by other fields, sits on the edge of town no further than a decent long clearance away from the main Pacific Highway between Sydney and Brisbane, with the ocean itself just a kilometre away to the other side.

The smattering of fans sat back, supped their beers and settled in for the expected crushing Australian victory under the floodlights. There was a merciful ten minute period at the start of the match when defiance was the appropriate adjective, as the young Nicky Salapu, promoted to captain in the absence of all of his regular national team colleagues, kept Australia at bay with a string of fine early saves, including an acrobatic tip over the bar from Aurelio Vidmar's shot. Such defiance could never last, and once the back line was first breached in the tenth minute by Con Boutsianis the floodgates didn't merely nudge open, they completely fell apart, smashed asunder by the onrushing Australian tide.

The goals rained in from all sides, all angles and in all manners. There were goals from neat flicks and towering headers. Goals from distance and from close in and at least a dozen, if not more, simple tap-ins. All the while, the luckless Nicky Salapu seemingly slumped further and further into despair; shorn of his regular teammates he was offered virtually no protection by the inexperienced, overawed, and frankly startled teenagers ahead of him. For a partisan sporting nation such as Australia, the crowd took the unusual step of switching cheers, if not allegiances, to their utterly outgunned opponents. American Samoans were cheered if they completed passes or made an interception and were treated to standing ovations at both half time and full time. Each save from Salapu, and there were a great many amongst the carnage, was met with applause as resounding as each Australian goal; his effort and ability appreciated despite its apparent fruitlessness and futility.

Perhaps not surprising given the haphazard way that the American Samoan team had finally come about, there was little cohesion, organisation or positional discipline amongst the collection of teenagers on the pitch. The short, or almost non-existent, preparation time had left a team seemingly under-coached and unprepared. They ran around chasing Australian shadows, drawn to the ball like moths to a flame, or like schoolboys in an unorganised kick about. Schoolboys is what most of them were, of course, young lambs to the slaughter, far out of their depth. According to Tony Langkilde, the team manager and Vice President of the Football Federation of American Samoa, some of those young lambs had never played a full ninety-minute game before. What chance did they have? They knew all along that anything other than defeat was impossible, but any chance at avoiding complete humiliation was long gone too.

In some ways, they didn't help their own cause. An almost suicidal 3-3-4 formation, even if most of the time it was barely apparent, was hardly designed to help matters. Having played that formation in the quiet, palm tree-lined surroundings of their home islands against

13

limited opposition, they saw little reason to alter it on this grander stage. Naïve in the extreme.

By half time no fewer than sixteen goals had found their way past Salapu, making for a somewhat tricky half time team talk in the American Samoan dressing room. 'It is very hard to pick your players up when they are so far behind at the interval,' was the incisive and acute understatement from Langkilde. 'The only real change I told them to make was to be more aggressive and alert and not to give the ball away so much,' he continued.[4] Sound advice I am sure, but not one that his players had the ability or the strength to carry out to any great effect, or any effect at all for that matter. And in the face of an opponent unwilling to step off the gas, the carnage continued unabated.

Having already hit Tonga for twenty-two a couple of days before, it was surely only a matter of time before even that staggering total was reached and surpassed in the second half. And so it proved. The momentous world record-breaking moment came in the 65th minute when Archie Thompson, a hitherto relative unknown in only his third appearance for the Australian national team, scored his eleventh goal of the match and the team's twenty-third. At 23-0 the world record they'd set only two days earlier had gone, but most alarmingly there were still twenty-five minutes to go.

In the final few minutes of the match, the Samoans let in so many goals, on occasion almost immediately following the previous restart, that the poor fellows in their shorts and tee-shirts who were operating the scoreboard lost count and erroneously awarded an extra goal to Australia. The stadium's scoreboard was not much more than a couple of guys with some plastic numbering, and they were kept on their toes throughout the night; far busier than the Australian defence, certainly. By the end, the scoreboard displayed the final score as 32-0; a bit of overenthusiasm on the part of its operators who had, in their excitement, apparently skipped straight from 27-0 to 29-0.

This naturally led to a bit of confusion as, by this point, most people had understandably lost count. FIFA stated that they would not officially confirm the result until reports from the referee and match commissioner had been received and checked. Once they had, the result was confirmed as 31-0 and Archie Thompson had bagged himself a whopping thirteen goals, and could comfortably have had one or two more. The Australians had scored at a rate of one goal every two minutes and forty-five seconds, which is a simply astonishing rate. When you consider the time taken up by thirty-one restarts by a team who must surely have been delaying each kick-off for as long as possible, the strike rate is even quicker in terms of actual playing time.

In amongst the endless Australian onslaught, American Samoa did manage the very occasional foray upfield. And on one glorious occasion they finally brought a save from the otherwise utterly unemployed Australian goalkeeper Michael Petkovic. In the 86th minute, and already 29-0 down, midfielder Pati Feagiai managed to send a weak shot in the direction of the Australian goal, prompting Petkovic to dive to his right to save it, as much to give himself something to do than for any necessity due to the ferociousness of the shot. It would be the only shot on goal managed by American Samoa all evening, and would be widely reported as the only time Petkovic touched the ball in the entire match. It was met with the biggest cheer of the night.

Archie Thompson's goal-scoring feat had not only comfortably beaten the previous World Cup scoring record but had utterly obliterated it. The record had stood at a measly six goals scored by Iran's Karim Bagheri in their aforementioned hammering of Guam. Now taking second place on that list of World Cup match goal-scorers was Thompson's Australian colleague David Zdrilic who had helped himself to eight goals in this match. He too had beaten the old world record and in other circumstances, this impressive feat would have propelled him to the forefront of the world's attention. Sadly for him, as it was his achievement would be nothing more than a mere side note in history thanks to Thompson's feat.

Thompson's thirteen goals were also the highest number in international football history, superseding the previous best of ten goals from almost a century before, jointly held by Denmark's Sophus Nielsen at the 1908 Olympic Games, and Germany's Gottfried Fuchs at the 1912 edition. Against what was effectively a youth team from a small Pacific Island, Archie Thompson's place in history was assured, although his place in the Australian team wasn't. The world record goal-scorer was not picked for their next match against Fiji a few days later. Given the furore regarding the American Samoan players' passports, it was a bitter irony that Archie Thompson was born in New Zealand to a kiwi father and a Papua New Guinean mother.

Thompson had only appeared twice before for his country and scored once prior to this match, having come onto the field towards the end of the big win over Tonga two days earlier to grab his first international goal. The big scorers on that day, strikers Damien Mori and John Aloisi, could only look on enviously from the bench on this occasion as Thompson rewrote the goal-scoring record books. 'Breaking the world record is a dream come true for me; that sort of thing doesn't come along every day,' he commented afterwards with a fair degree of stating the obvious. 'But you have to look at the teams we are playing and start asking questions. We don't need to play these games.'[5]

The general consensus of the powers that be seemed to be in agreement. FIFA's Director of Communications, Keith Cooper, commented: 'There doesn't seem to be much point in playing these kinds of matches. It doesn't do anyone any good.' Australian coach Frank Farina agreed, with a few strong words on the subject: 'No one really wins. It's a disgrace, embarrassing.'[6]

With all sporting hope gone, the American Samoans' faith allowed them a sense of perspective even in the face of such a bruising defeat. 'We were asking the Lord to help keep the score down,' the coach Tunoa Lui said afterwards. 'We will work at it and try to improve. God is the righteous one and, because of him, losing by so many goals does not matter.'[7]

But was the extent of the beating entirely necessary? Just what did Australia have to prove by carrying on the brutal massacre long after the victory was well assured? Tony Langkilde felt Australia could, and perhaps should, have taken their foot off the gas in the second half in particular. 'For the game's integrity I thought they would have,' he lamented afterwards. Tunoa Lui, agreed: 'We don't know what Australia were trying to prove scoring all those goals. They have a different mind, they had probably targeted the record from the start and there was nothing we could do about it,' he despaired. 'They could have eased up. They didn't need those goals.'[8]

In apparent agreement with this sentiment, the club manager of two of the Australian players involved, Dick Advocaat, who managed Craig Moore and Tony Vidmar at Glasgow Rangers at the time, dropped both players from their next club match because of their perceived unsportsmanlike conduct.

There was of course no obligation on Australia to do anything other than win the game by as great a margin as possible. Farina went back on his initial scathing assessment of the worth of the match in praising his players' 'professional attitude' and going about the victory in 'a very professional manner'. 'It's a result and really, that's all that matters,' he added.[9]

But given the huge disparity between the strongest and weakest teams in the Oceania region, this resounding thrashing did at least prompt something of a rethink with regards to the World Cup qualifying format. The smaller, weaker nations would go into a pre-qualifying group for subsequent tournaments. 'I don't think this will happen again,' Keith Cooper added. 'It's quite clear none of the other confederations have such a gap between the top and bottom.'[10] Indeed, FIFA's own code of Fair Play tells all its teams to 'respect your adversaries,' which is something of a catch-all statement but could be interpreted as suggesting that teams don't humiliate the opposition to quite this extent, even if they are officially the worst team in the world.

Humiliated and humbled, American Samoa had just provided the most compelling and conclusive evidence for the accuracy of their lowly world ranking. As the Australian crowd warmly and sympathetically applauded their beaten opponents, the American Samoans were just starting to come to terms with having suffered the worst defeat in international football history, and by some margin. The 31-0 defeat would make them a laughing stock, gaining them an unwanted place on many an 'and finally…' segment of numerous global news outlets, as the world's press treated them to repeated headlines focusing on the scoreline. Amongst the majority of headlines making use of the phrase "smash world record" at least *The Telegraph*'s cricket-related stab at mocking the American Samoans had a hint of humour about it, albeit still piling on the humiliation: "Australia score 31 without loss."

Such a beating leaves scars on its victims. Deep, psychological scars that would remain etched in the minds of some. The consequences of this defeat would linger with them, and indeed haunt them. None suffered more than the hapless Nicky Salapu who would carry the demons with him for years. Emotional wounds that would be opened again and again as his name became synonymous with the defeat. In spite of picking the ball out of his net 31 times, Salapu had, incredibly, done more than any of his team mates to keep the score down, yet couldn't escape his thoughts that this was 'the worst thing ever'. As heavy a defeat as it was, it could easily have been so much worse but for Salapu's saves; around 20 in all. Described by his manager as 'a very brave keeper' who 'kept the score down with a magnificent display', he had flung himself from pillar to post, desperately trying to stem the tide amidst the devastation in front of him.

As the final whistle finally brought an end to his suffering and his teammates sang to the slightly bemused Australian crowd, Salapu's expression revealed the burden he already knew he would have to carry. As well as he'd played, he would forever be 'the man who conceded all those goals'. He would return to his home in Seattle to be reminded of this match at every turn. Any conversation about American Samoa would inexorably lead to the question, 'Oh, are you the guy that gave up thirty-one goals?' His son was teased about it at school.

Salapu himself would seek to exorcise the demons by repeatedly taking on Australia on his PlayStation, scoring goal after goal for American Samoa against an unmanned opposition, the second controller sitting idly by his side.

The defeat confirmed American Samoa's place at the foot of the FIFA rankings of course, but Langkilde felt that situation wouldn't last. 'We will get better by the match,' he said optimistically. 'But despite what some people say I refuse to accept that we are the worst team in the world. Yes, we are the newest team on FIFA's list, but we will prove over the next couple of years that we are not the worst.'[11] Tunoa Lui concurred, citing that football development in American Samoa was on the increase, aided in no small part by FIFA grants now that they were in the governing body's club, so to speak. 'We are in the second year of the sport being played in elementary and high schools and have a very good under-15 side. In five years we will be competitive.'[12] That would prove to be rather inaccurate, unsurprisingly.

American Samoa completed their World Cup qualifying campaign with a 5-0 defeat to a Tonga side who were no doubt thoroughly relieved to have had their own world record defeat usurped so quickly. In all, 57 goals were conceded by Nicky Salapu in the four matches, with no goals scored. They did at least score in the following year's OFC Nations Cup, but their two goals against Tonga on that occasion came in a 7-2 defeat. That match did at least mark the first time they'd ever scored in an official FIFA sanctioned fixture, some small consolation perhaps. But the heavy defeats just kept on coming: 10-0 to New Caledonia in 2002, 9-1 to Vanuatu in 2004, 11-0 to Fiji, 10-0 to Papua New Guinea, 15-0 to Vanuatu again. Life can be very hard for those at the bottom, and even more so when they are pitted against vastly superior opposition. Sadly for American Samoa - the worst team in the world in the early twentieth century - any opposition could be classed as vastly superior.

As Langkilde lamented: 'Football is a game of three possibilities: win, tie and loss. For us it is only a game of one possibility: loss. We have not had the other two possibilities yet.'[13]

* * * * *

Since the FIFA rankings first came into use in late 1992, things have never been easy for those stuck at the bottom. Prior to the rankings first taking effect, any previous disastrous runs of form or multiple thrashings were partly hidden from the wider world. Until the rankings came into being, nobody suffered the label of being the worst in the world. That changed as soon as the first table was published in December 1992.

The team with the ignominy of being highlighted as the inaugural official worst national team in the world was the Chinese Special Administrative Region of Macau. This dubious honour was bestowed on Macau in spite of recording a win over Chinese Taipei the previous June in Asian Cup qualification. When the subsequent rankings came out – not until August 1993 – Macau were joint-last with the Maldives, but it was Macau who would remain rooted to the bottom for nigh on the next three years as other teams came and went.

As if seeking to confirm this status, Macau set about proving their label correct in a particularly diligent and conscientious manner. In the Asian zone qualification for the 1994 World Cup, Macau succumbed to six defeats from six matches, and by no small margin either. A 10-1 thrashing by Kuwait would provide the only occasion Macau managed to score a goal, with a 9-0 loss to Malaysia and a couple of 8-0 defeats to Saudi Arabia and Kuwait added in for good measure. They wouldn't play again for almost three years, leaving them firmly stuck in the basement. Their return to action wasn't hugely better, losing to their big brother, the People's Republic of China, 7-1 in an Asian Cup qualifier, though that qualifying tournament would finally see them rise above the bottom gaining a result against the Philippines.

Another Asian nation down on their luck in the early years of the world rankings were actually a former power of the Asian game in the 1960s and early 1970s. Admittedly, that's not a startling claim to fame in global terms, but nonetheless the national team of the Khmer Republic, as Cambodia was previously known, enjoyed a period of relative success during that era. Having been exposed to the game in the early twentieth century, much earlier than many other Asian nations – a 'benefit' of their French colonial past – football in Cambodia gradually gained popularity. Consequently, when many other countries in the region were still only taking up the game, Cambodian football was well organised and reached its peak with a fourth place finish in the 1972 Asian Cup. Unfortunately for them there were no world rankings in those halcyon days to record and reflect this success.

But as civil war and the overspill from the Vietnam conflict segued into the brutal realities of the Khmèr Rouge regime under Pol Pot, football understandably became utterly unimportant. All football development was set back to zero as the country and its people were changed forever. It wasn't until the 1990s when Cambodia would fully rejoin the football world as the long road to ruin and recovery meant that the national team didn't play between 1974 and 1995. Once that comeback occurred, in the South East Asian Games in December 1995, the tradition of footballing ability and relative regional excellence was long gone. What remained was a team of players who had grown up with greater worries than honing their skills with a ball. The net result when Cambodia appeared on the world rankings for the first time? A stint as the world's worst.

That South East Asian Games campaign went understandably badly. At least things improved after their opening 10-0 defeat to Indonesia though. They lost their next match by the relatively close score-line of 4-0 to their neighbours Vietnam, before swiftly reverting to type with two 9-0 thrashings inflicted by Malaysia and Thailand. Back in the footballing fold they may have been, but they were understandably out of their depth.

Such regular thrashings aren't exclusive to the more exotic corners of the earth, however, as Europe has its own minnows suffering regular and repeated humiliation on the football field. In Europe, some of the strongest national teams in the world sit, literally in many cases, side-by-side with some of the weakest. Spain and France surround Andorra. Liechtenstein borders Switzerland and Austria and is just a few mountains away from both Germany and Italy. Luxembourg borders Germany, France and Belgium. Then there's Gibraltar - UEFA members only rather than a FIFA affiliate - not much more than a rock hanging from the southern tip of Spain. But traditionally the weakest of them all is San Marino, surrounded by the footballing behemoth than is Italy.

Even before finally succumbing to the inevitable and hitting rock bottom of the rankings in 2008, San Marino had become a byword for the futility of sporting mismatches to most European observers. Their record defeat, one that came almost a year before reaching FIFA's bottom rung, was a defeat to the mighty Germany in Euro 2008 qualification. The thirteen goals that nestled in Aldo Simoncini's net that night were a humiliation for him and his country, and yet pale into relative insignificance when compared to some of the heaviest defeats meted out in other regions.

Having hit rock bottom, San Marino naturally continued to lose, but never by quite such a margin again. There was a seemingly endless stream of defeats though: 10-0 to Poland, 11-0 to the Netherlands, 9-0 to Ukraine, and a few eight-goal defeats including against England. The usual reaction to such margins of defeat from the rest of Europe was a shake of the head, and a muttering along the lines of "Just what is the point?" Perhaps more chastening for San Marino than those defeats were the times they lost to a team that was potentially beatable. The likes of Liechtenstein and Malta also beat San Marino during their lengthy spell as the worst in the world; narrow one-goal defeats that must have felt like real opportunities missed and potentially a greater frustration than losing heavily to the high and mighty.

By virtue of their geography, and the current set up of European qualification for both the World Cup and European Championship, San Marino will remain permanently outclassed, fighting to delay the onset of inevitable defeat on almost every occasion they take to the field. They have developed, though, enough nous and experience to usually avoid the score-line heading off into cricket-match territory even when faced with truly world-class opposition. That is a claim that the likes of American Samoa certainly couldn't make, in spite of the considerably lower standard of opponent they generally faced.

When it comes to being hopelessly out of their depth, we return to the 2002 World Cup qualification, which was an all-round bad one for the far-flung minnows of world football. As American Samoa failed to stem the constant tide of Socceroo attacks, so another of America's Pacific island territories was suffering their own mauling. As mentioned earlier, prior to Australia's rampaging victories in Coffs Harbour, Guam were the previous holders of the worst defeat in World Cup history. Their own night of shame had come while they sat just above the foot of the world rankings, sitting atop only American Samoa and Montserrat at the time. Placed in a first round group in the Asian zone of World Cup qualifying alongside Tajikistan and one of Asian football's giants, Iran, they held little hope of progressing. But Karim Bagheri's six goals led Iran to a 19-0 win in the group's opening match, before Tajikistan compounded the misery inflicting a 16-0 thumping on poor Guam. They would reach a new low with a 21-0 loss to North Korea in the 2005 East Asian Championships, after which they were presumably eternally grateful for Australia's record-breaking wins over Tonga and American Samoa.

Humbling defeats need not only come courtesy of a resounding goal margin though. Being beaten by a team that is of equally low standing would be just as humbling for a nation from the depths of the world rankings. With that in mind, the 2002 World Cup would provide the backdrop for one of the rare occasions when two teams from world football's basement would meet each other. Dubbed 'The Other Final', and played on the same day as the real World Cup Final in Japan, the clash between Bhutan and Montserrat would briefly focus attention on the wrong end of world football's meritocracy.

Worst in the World

Chapter 2: The Other Final

The pitch high up in the Himalayas was nothing more than patchy grass interspersed with murky brown puddles, but for such a momentous occasion the surrounding stadium had been dressed up a treat. For an hour before kick-off in the Changlimithang Stadium in Thimphu, Bhutan, an array of ornately attired dancers, all gold, blue and red and everything in between, performed their traditional dragon dances to the hypnotic metronome beat resonating from the blue clad drummers.

Reams of coloured flags and banners lined the touchlines creating a rather picturesque setting, behind which the crowds sat in neat rows on the grassy banks, or for the lucky few, on the grubby concrete benches of the main stand. Tall housing blocks loomed behind them providing a fine view for some. Opposite the main stand, the ornate Royal Pavilion sits serenely observing proceedings, providing entertainment and comfort for the elite. Even in these humble surroundings, and at this level of international football, the hospitality was still present. The pavilion is backed by sharply rising grassy peaks, from which several housing blocks sprout through the greenery affording their residents a terrific view of the action unfolding below.

The crowds of locals on the grass banks provided a colourful scene. All dressed in traditional dress, the *gho* - a knee length robe somewhat resembling a kimono, tied at the waist with a belt – many had brought bright umbrellas to shield them from the sun. The opened umbrellas created a rainbow effect, which was further enhanced by the coloured banners draped from the buildings behind. It was *the* event in town and all of Bhutanese society was there to witness it: from the President and other VIPs in their tents, to the glamorous women sitting high in the stands, to the local workers and their young and frequently face-painted children. Some spectators sat even higher, scattered far and wide in amongst the trees and bushes in the hills a little further back. Everyone wanted to be a part of the occasion and to see this historic match. It was an event the likes of which Bhutanese football had never seen.

In many ways it, of course, bore no relation to the real World Cup final of 2002 taking place in Yokohama on the same day, but in others it had all the pageantry, atmosphere, and sense of occasion that befits a global football event. That such an event took place, between the two lowliest ranked nations in world football at the time, was entirely thanks to an enterprising Dutch film crew who turned their nation's disappointment at failing to qualify for the 2002 World Cup into an idea to look at those national teams rather more accustomed to losing than their own. This idea took them to the FIFA website and its world rankings.

'There are many countries which are used to losing a lot…at the far bottom of this list you find Bhutan and Montserrat,' explained one of the Dutch filmmakers, Matthijs de Jongh. 'Then what we did, it was a bit naïve maybe, was to send two faxes, one to Montserrat and one to Bhutan, and then we just waited for a reaction.'[14]

Those faxes arrived in the respective football association headquarters of Montserrat and Bhutan. One headquarters was nothing more than a house surrounded by the lush vegetation of a tropical island with only the sign outside to identify it as a national FA epicentre, while the other was a sparsely furnished, wood-panelled office from which emanated the calmness and serenity of a Buddhist temple. Both Football Associations were receptive to the idea; a rare and privileged chance, albeit a dubious one, to perform on an international stage far beyond what was generally available to either nation's teams.

'I said to myself, 'Well, hey, this is a great experience and something that we can really look forward to," declared Charles Thompson, a member of the Montserrat police force and captain of the national team. Meanwhile in Bhutan, none other than the country's Prime Minister, Lyongo Khandu Wangchuk, summed up his nation's positive response: 'We felt there was an opportunity where in some way or the other we could participate in the biggest world sporting event. It would provide our country and our team an opportunity to share our love for the game.'[15]

Agreements in place, the film makers set about making hasty arrangements for the match which would become the focal point of their documentary film, *The Other Final*, and would answer definitively the question of which was the worst national team in the world at that time.

Of the two teams, it was the tiny Caribbean island of Montserrat who sat at the bottom of the rankings ahead of the match. Little more than a tear-shaped dot on the map in the Leeward Islands chain of the Caribbean Sea, more or less equidistant between Antigua, St Kitts and Guadeloupe, Montserrat is a British Overseas Territory of only a few thousand people. One of football's smallest national associations, Montserrat had only been a member of FIFA for three years at the time, having joined in 1999. Since then they had played a mere handful of official matches, and lost them all. Immediately after joining the FIFA fold, they lost a two-legged playoff to the less than mighty British Virgin Islands in the preliminary round of the 1999 Caribbean Cup, although the score lines were kept to respectable levels: 3-1 and 3-0 defeats. They did suffer though from having to play both legs in the British Virgin Islands' capital Road Town for reasons we'll come on to shortly.

Their years before FIFA affiliation had brought the occasional victory. Very occasional in fact, as there were just two of them, both against the fellow British Overseas Territory and only marginally less tiny island of Anguilla. They even managed a draw against Anguilla once also; an unprecedented level of success for Montserrat. Their reward for having beaten Anguilla home and away in the 1995 Caribbean Cup first qualifying round was a meeting with the significantly more densely populated island nation of St Vincent and the Grenadines. It's all relative of course, St Vincent is a tiny country by most people's reckoning and a real minnow of world football as a result, but compared to Montserrat they are something of a Goliath.

Those encounters with St Vincent constituted Montserrat's final matches before becoming a fully-fledged FIFA affiliated nation, in spite of taking place four years ahead of receiving FIFA recognition. But the two-legged playoff with St Vincent and the Grenadines didn't go well. A 9-0 defeat away from home was followed by an 11-0 humiliation at their home ground of Sturge Park in Plymouth; what was at the time the capital of Montserrat.

FIFA recognition in 1999 altered little in Montserrat's fruitless search for triumph on the football field. The defeats kept on coming, and by 2002 Montserrat had lost all five of their officially recognised international matches, plus another against the non-FIFA affiliated French arrondissement of Saint-Martin. Given Montserrat's tiny population, around 5,000 in 2002, achieving much more than merely losing respectably would be viewed as quite a success. With only one hundred and fifty amateur players registered with the five teams in Montserrat's national league, the pickings were at best slim for the national team coach, Englishman Paul Morris; a policeman like his captain Charles Thompson.

Morris had learned the football coaching ropes alongside his prior police work during his time as part of London's Metropolitan Police. He moved to Montserrat for a more sedate way of life, but his previous coaching knowledge meant he was one of the more experienced football coaches on the island, and a step into the realm of international football became his. Morris' trips home usually saw him returning with various bits of football equipment, from kit to corner flags to referees' whistles. Such supplies just can't be found on Montserrat so everything had to be brought in from elsewhere.

Added to that logistical stumbling block is the fact that football is not the sport of choice for the majority of Montserratians. That distinction belongs to the more genteel past time of cricket, and so it is perhaps no surprise that they found themselves struggling in the football rankings. Montserrat's first foray into the World Cup, in the preliminary round of regional qualification for the 2002 tournament, saw them beaten twice by the Dominican Republic and exiting at the earliest opportunity. The home leg was again played away from Montserrat, in Port of Spain, Trinidad, on that occasion.

During the period of their FIFA recognition, football has hardly been the number one priority for the people of Montserrat. There had been hurricanes and earthquakes, but worst of all the regular eruptions of the Soufrière Hills volcano had a devastating and long lasting impact on both the island and its people. These eruptions are also the reason for Montserrat's nomadic home venues in both the aforementioned 2002 World Cup qualifiers and the 1999 Caribbean Cup losses to the British Virgin Islands, as they destroyed the national stadium along with so much else.

After lying dormant for hundreds of years, Soufrière Hills became active in 1995 and continued to erupt thereafter with devastating regularity over the subsequent few years. The volcano spewed its poisonous and devastating pyroclastic flows of terrifyingly hot gases, ash and rocks in all directions, swiftly pouring down and suffocating the nearby towns, the capital Plymouth included. Plymouth had been initially evacuated in 1995, but was fully abandoned a couple of years later; a ghost town by then destroyed and submerged under several metres of ash, like a modern-day Pompeii.[16]

Nigh on half of Montserrat was devastated, leaving much of the island formerly known as an "Emerald Isle" now resembling a barren lunar landscape. The island's population was devastated too. An unlucky few were killed by the poisonous hot gases, but many thousands left the island during the evacuation and chose not to return. In all, nearly two-thirds of the island's population of about 11,500 left Montserrat, many to neighbouring Antigua and around 4,000 to the UK, with only 5,000 or so remaining.

Amongst the devastation, the national stadium, Sturge Park, was destroyed like everything else in Plymouth, and by 2002 it lay under several metres of ash, cut off from the rest of the island. Naturally, it would be in no condition for football for an awful many years to come, situated as it was in 2002, and still is today, in the exclusion zone that the southern end of Montserrat had become. Like many of the island's inhabitants, Charles Thompson, the national team captain, suffered greatly from the eruption, losing not one but two properties in Plymouth. His story was not an unusual one of course. As well as property lost, many friends and family of those who remained in Montserrat had moved elsewhere. Little wonder then that Thompson could neatly sum up the feelings of most of the islanders when he lamented that the volcanic crisis 'disrupted my entire life.'[17]

In 2002, the island was very much still limping to recovery, most of its infrastructure and income sources having vanished into dust. As Montserrat's football players prepared for their clash with Bhutan a couple of years after the worst of the eruptions had ended, the island was almost totally reliant on British aid. From a footballing point of view, Montserrat's recovery was aided by FIFA's GOAL programme, a charitable project launched by the ever-controversial FIFA President Sepp Blatter in 1999 to 'allow each member association of FIFA to receive funding for football development projects that respond to the special needs of their national associations.'[18] It is thanks to such schemes that Blatter, for all his controversies, remains such a popular figure amongst the smaller members of FIFA who are in receipt of FIFA's benevolence. In Montserrat's case, its inclusion in the GOAL programme allowed the development of a new national stadium in Blakes, to the north of the island, and provided funding for various youth development and educational schemes. Against the backdrop of this assisted recovery, the clash with Bhutan now meant that 'the world is watching a truly resilient people rise from the ashes,' as noted by the Team Manager Claude Hogan.[19]

While the new facility began to take shape, training, and indeed most friendly kick-abouts in Montserrat, took place on a rather scenic but basic pitch. The bumpy, lush pitch was surrounded by a ramshackle fence and flanked on either side by steep green hills with the ocean never too far away. There were no changing rooms, showers or any other facilities. The hills on either side were overgrown with deep, thick greenery, so much so that any stray strike which missed the crumbling, rusting goalposts would lead to a prolonged search for the ball, buried somewhere in the undergrowth. Added to that was the ever-present chance of ash particles lingering in the air from the still brooding volcano, making for stinging eyes and difficulty in breathing. The new FIFA-funded facilities would improve some of those conditions at least, if not all.

Depicted in the film, *The Other Final*, the now disgraced former President of CONCACAF Jack Warner is pictured at the opening of phase one of the new stadium. When questioned about the upcoming clash with Bhutan he was typically bullish: 'Caribbean football is similar to our dance, our music, our carnival, our calypso, and is peculiar to this region. Asian football is not comparable to Caribbean football. It doesn't have the flair and the panache that you get in the Caribbean,' he enthused. 'Montserrat will leave the last place in the ranking as soon as they have beaten Bhutan. And Montserrat will beat Bhutan come June, and show them that the last place they were holding was only temporary.'[20] Fighting talk from the confederation's head honcho, but of course you would expect nothing less.

Almost nine thousand miles to the east, and significantly higher above sea level, Bhutan were of course hoping to avoid descending to that last place in the ranking. At the time, they were one of the youngest members of world football's governing body, having joined a year later than Montserrat in 2000. Like Montserrat, they'd lost all of their official matches since joining FIFA, but in an era when ranking points were awarded for losses too, the fact that Bhutan were beaten by a higher class of opponent had kept them narrowly off the bottom.

They weren't spared a few brutal beatings however, and in their first venture into the qualifying rounds of the Asian Cup in 2000 they suffered a then world record defeat to Kuwait, a match described by Bhutanese striker Dinesh Chhetri as 'quite a bitter experience.'[21] He wasn't wrong there. Twenty goals found their way into the Bhutan net as the Kuwaitis showed no mercy. Even the Kuwaiti goalkeeper, no doubt thoroughly bored through inactivity, took and scored a late penalty to record goal number nineteen. In the same group, they also contrived to lose by eight goals to Turkmenistan and nine goals to Yemen, though they did at least find the net twice in an 11-2 defeat.

Even before their FIFA days, Bhutan hadn't managed to avoid defeat even once. Three entries into the South East Asian Games football tournament in the 1980s resulted in a return home with nothing but defeat to their name on each occasion. Those experiences seemingly scarred them to such a great degree that the football federation withdrew the national team from the international stage for the next twelve years, only resurfacing again in 1999 to once again travel to the South East Asian Games. Their absence hadn't done anything to improve their prospects however, as once again they lost all three of their matches. The only saving grace was to be found in a one-goal defeat to Pakistan, which suggested there may be some small ray of hope for the future. This footballing isolation is a recurring theme for Bhutan as prior to the 2018 World Cup qualifying process, in which they did compete, they were the only country in FIFA never to have taken part in the World Cup qualifying.

Football hasn't been played for very long in Bhutan, a nation that had remained splendidly isolated from the world until the mid-1970s. Bhutan is one of the most unspoiled Himalayan areas, a country of ancient monasteries, fluttering prayer flags and breath-taking mountainous natural beauty. A country where almost every aspect of life is deeply influenced by Buddhism since its arrival from Tibet in the seventh century, with monks having ruled the country for centuries until an absolute monarchy was established in 1907. It has the noble distinction of having been independent throughout its entire history, existing more or less in its current form from relatively recently when various warring fiefdoms united as one in the nineteenth century.

Bhutan remained untouched by foreign influence until 1974 when its closely guarded policy of isolationism was slowly, gradually lifted. King Jigme Singye Wangchuk 'opened a chink into the world's best-kept secret,' as noted in a *Daily Telegraph* travel article, with its borders opened up for the first occasion in modern times. Since then a modicum of international influence and a highly regulated trickle of tourists have been allowed in, providing the country with its second largest source of revenue – 'after hydro-electric power and just ahead of postage stamps.'[22]

Several photos of the King, who has since abdicated in 2006 in favour of his son, adorned the sparse offices of the Bhutan Football Federation in 2002. Prime among them was one depicting the young King some decades earlier leaning down to pick up a ball from in front of a goal. In his youth, it seems the King was quite the goalkeeper. Once the country had opened up to some level of development, something that it is still extremely guarded about – it remains to this day the only country in the world to shun the use of traffic lights – many Bhutanese went to study in neighbouring countries, notably India. There they were exposed to football and once they returned to Bhutan on finishing their education, they brought football with them. What they didn't bring was much coaching expertise.

One such travelling student was Wangyel Dorji, captain of the national team in 2002, who told the filmmakers: 'In my early school days we always played football. Just for joy. We never had proper training, just went to the field and kicked the ball here and there. Of course, I played football from a very early age, but not in a scientific way. Then in 1996 when I was studying in India I got selected for one of the football academies in India.'[23] Dorji dreamt of one day playing for Arsenal - 'I know I can't, but I can dream' – and was one of only nine hundred amateur players in a country where the national sporting passions are stirred more by archery, a festival event attracting competitors from every town and village, than they are the beautiful game.

What the Bhutanese are also interested in is the pursuit of a rather unique philosophy aimed at achieving gross national happiness, to which the country and its government has been committed for some time. As explained by the Minister of Foreign Affairs, Lyongo Thinley: 'It is based on the realisation of the truth that every human being searches for happiness in life. That is the ultimate goal. And if it is the ultimate goal of every Bhutanese, every human being, then it becomes the responsibility of the government.'[24]

Such a concept has developed from the Bhutanese grounding in Buddhist ideals, and since the country opened itself up to the outside world in the last forty years it has 'gained an almost mythical status as a real-life Shangri-La,' as wistfully described in an article in the *Guardian*.[25] This ideal suggests that the most beneficial model for the development of society comes when material and spiritual development take place side by side, complementing each other. Uniquely in the world, Bhutan rejects Gross National Product as the only means of measuring its prosperity and instead measures its Gross National Happiness by focusing on four particular formal principles: the promotion of sustainable and equitable development, the preservation and promotion of cultural and spiritual values, conservation of the natural environment, and the establishment of good governance.[26]

Sadly, their football team hadn't been a great source of enhancing the Bhutanese people's happiness given their woeful results over the years, but in a typically measured Buddhist fashion, even the world of competitive sport can be viewed in terms of the material and spiritual taking place side by side. The Minister of Foreign Affairs once more: 'I think there are two dimensions to the world of sports. One is the opportunity that it gives to individuals and countries, to communities, for social and cultural interaction. And that, I think, is the most important contribution that sports can make to society,' he commented in *The Other Final*, putting a clear emphasis on these less tangible benefits than on sporting victory. Just as well, for a supporter of Bhutanese football, you might well say.

'The other dimension is the world of competition, and the world of success and failure,' he continued. 'Unfortunately I think that success and failure in sport have become the most important. For me the world of sports as a means to promote understanding and friendship among people is far more important than the world of rivalry and battles that sports promote.'[27] This outlook was very much in keeping with the underlying idea behind this match. Yes, of course both teams harboured dreams of performing well and winning, but both were equally focused on the experience and opportunity for two very different cultures to meet through their shared love of football.

'Because of this sports event every Bhutanese will now know where Montserrat is,' Lyongo Thinley added ahead of the match. 'And they will, I am sure, have love and respect and understanding for that country, irrespective of whether we win or lose because that is why we have agreed to play the game.'[28] Bhutan's Football Federation's general secretary concurred, commenting: 'We are doing this because we are part of the global football family. We're happy to play Montserrat.'[29]

Montserrat's Claude Hogan called the benefits of learning about another culture as 'the most important thing' to be gained from the whole experience. 'Winning, of course,' he added, 'will be a bonus.'[30] But his team had to get to Bhutan first; a laborious process involving no fewer than seven flights. Even escaping the Caribbean seemed an almost terminally complex endeavour as a flight from Montserrat to Antigua was followed by an onward connection to St Martin and then Curacao. From that former Dutch colony they finally crossed the Atlantic to Amsterdam and on to Bangkok, Calcutta and then eventually Thimphu, almost a week after they set off from home. It was as though they were still unsure just where Bhutan was, as they dotted around the world on a variety of bearings before finally heading in the right direction.

They departed Montserrat to the strains of the song 'Hot, Hot, Hot' playing over local radio to see them on their way; a global hit for one of Montserrat's most famous sons who performed under the stage name Arrow. The song's later incarnation as a Pizza Hut advert should bring it to mind for those unfamiliar with soca music hits of the 1980s. The song became the de facto anthem for the Montserrat national team, and would be heard repeatedly throughout their adventure to Bhutan.

In *The Other Final*, the squad are depicted attempting their own version of the song whilst waiting for the fifth flight of their journey in an Amsterdam departure lounge. Goalkeeper Cecil Lake gets his keyboard out and gives the singing a decent stab, but the others seem rather more reluctant and mumble their way through like a bunch of schoolboys forced to sing in assembly by an overenthusiastic teacher. Having finally arrived in Thimphu, after a weather-induced delay in Calcutta where several players went down with food poisoning, they stepped off the plane to be greeted with, and overwhelmed by, numerous gifts from their welcoming hosts. Another rendition of 'Hot, Hot, Hot' on the bus from the airport to their hotel received a rather more favourable response, as the relief at the torturous journey finally reaching its conclusion was palpable.

There were still seven days to go until the match, but having taken the best part of a week to get there, the team needed to adjust to their new surroundings. Firstly, and perhaps most importantly, they had to get used to being at high altitude – Thimphu sits at roughly 8,500 feet above sea level – and secondly they had to overcome their various Calcutta-induced ailments. These factors in particular meant that acclimatisation, recovery and training time was very much of the essence.

Both teams' final preparations also took place with new coaches at the helm. Montserrat's Paul Morris had quit just days before departure in protest over selection interference from above, while Bhutan's previous coach had died suddenly. Montserrat went for a local solution in William Lewis, but Bhutan brought in a Dutchman, Arie Schans, who had been coaching at amateur level in the Netherlands. He brought a more professional attitude and more advanced methods with him, and Bhutan's training in the days prior to the match was rather more focused than that of their Montserrat counterparts.

The visiting islanders had plenty of reason for distraction however; they were half a world away from their native land with the novelty of being in a distinct, contrasting and downright unusual environment. In addition, the Montserrat players were subject to far more interest than they could have imagined, or indeed ever have experienced. Strolling through the streets of Thimphu, the squad made for quite an intimidating sight, particularly given how most of them stood head and shoulders above the locals. They were such big news in Bhutan that the Montserrat players found themselves regularly mobbed and pestered for autographs.

As match day approached, the enormity of it all began to weigh heavily on some. It had become newsworthy around the world by this time, but for those players gathered in Bhutan the expectation was growing, as was the sense of wanting to perform to their best and not let anyone down.

It wasn't only the two teams who were going through their final preparations, as the stadium itself was undergoing something of a spruce up. Little could be done to rectify the patchwork grass or the numerous puddles of mud, but the grass such as it was, was kept in check by a gang of women all dressed in the traditional kira, long woven cloth dresses covered by silk jackets. They clipped away optimistically at the rogue blades of grass with mini sickles, their children dutifully following them around the pitch.

A harassed looking middle-aged man wandered from one penalty area to the other applying paint by hand from a bucket, and I mean that literally – there were no paint brushes being used – to mark out the pitch. One penalty spot was in the middle of one of the larger brown puddles, and the poor put-upon groundsman built up layer upon layer of powdered paint to create a small white island of a penalty spot amidst its murky brown surroundings. He splashed through the water in paint-splattered flip-flops while his rather more elegantly attired female assistant carried the paint bucket at arm's length, trying valiantly to keep her sodden footwear clear of the paint.

The stadium itself, undeniably one of the more scenic national stadiums in world football, was also worlds apart from its World Cup final equivalent in Japan. No modern high banks of double-tiered seating, no bowl shape surrounding the pitch, no rubber running track keeping the players at some distance from those watching. Rather, the Changlimithang Stadium sits among the Himalayan peaks of Thimphu, built on the site of an 1885 battle; one of the decisive battles of Bhutanese history which established the supremacy of the first monarch of Bhutan and led to unification. The stadium was completed in 1974 for the coronation of King Jigme Wangchuk, the goalkeeping monarch mentioned earlier. While football is the main use of this particular part of the stadium, the next-door archery ground is in more frequent use with regular tournaments held, often featuring traditional bamboo bows and a great deal of traditional song and dance.

But football was the order of the day on this occasion, and the teams marched onto the pitch watched by what must surely have been the largest crowd any of them had ever played in front of. Opinions vary on just how many were there, but the range is generally cited as being somewhere between 10,000 and 15,000 in attendance. Wherever the truth sits, one thing is certain: the number of people watching the match was at the very least double the population of Montserrat. To counter their likely feelings of being severely outnumbered, the intrepid islanders did at least have some support in the stadium. Thousands of schoolchildren were dressed in the colours of the two teams: Montserrat's green as well as Bhutan's yellow and orange. As the players made their way onto the field, the crowd broke into their own brief rendition of 'Hot, Hot, Hot,' as a pleasant welcome to their visitors.

As if buoyed by their welcome, Montserrat kicked off and had the best of the very early moments with strikers Bob Morris and Vladimir Farrell both forcing neat, diving saves from the Bhutan keeper. But that initial flurry was not to last long as Bhutan began to take over. Only four minutes were on the clock when they took the lead as a fluffed clearance from a Bhutanese corner looped towards the head of Wangyel Dorji, who needed no further invitation to nod his team ahead, though his glanced header barely made it across the line. It was a goal befitting the clash of the two worst teams in the world: a poor clearance, a weak header at goal and an aimless flap at the air as the ball travelled slowly past him by the Montserrat goalkeeper, Cecil Lake.

Montserrat tried to keep up their early tempo as the tackles began to fly in, but their efforts came to nought in the second half as Dorji banged in a second with a well-taken free kick, and that was swiftly followed by a third from Dinesh Chhetri. As each strike nestled behind him in the net, Cecil Lake's despondency plunged to further depths: at one point he tore his gloves off and threw them to the ground in frustration, then after another Bhutanese goal he sat slumped against his goal post for a long, desolate minute. As the game wore on and reached its latter stages, Montserrat's play had become increasingly ragged. The combined effects of altitude, extensive travel, and their missing coach finally took their toll, resulting in an increasingly dispirited display.

Dorji completed his hat trick late on to finish the game 4-0 and to confirm Montserrat as the undisputed worst national team in the world. The final whistle brought noisy Bhutanese celebrations in the crowd and on the pitch, as the jubilant players hoisted their coach aloft before embarking on a celebratory lap of honour, hand in hand with each other.

Meanwhile, Cecil Lake trudged glumly, head down, to join his teammates in commiseration. But soon both teams were arm in arm, embracing, congratulating, consoling and consolidating friendships and making a public display of the value that sport, and football in particular, can bring.

There was even a trophy, less glittering, less golden, less valuable, and certainly less revered than the one lifted by Brazilian captain Cafu in Yokohama a few hours later, but just reward nonetheless. Dorji wouldn't lift it alone however, preferring to share the moment with Charles Thompson, his beaten counterpart, as the formalities segued into a full-on party for players and public alike, culminating in both teams watching the World Cup final together later that evening.

'It feels great,' was Wangyel Dorji's elated reaction. 'Montserrat played well but the altitude seemed to be their weakness.' The effects of the altitude were of course very real, and were also mentioned by Charles Thompson in his assessment of events: 'We played really hard and we accept defeat. The altitude was a big factor and the conditions we are unaccustomed to,' he said. 'We'd like the chance for Bhutan to come to our place and play there.'[31]

Chance would be a fine thing. As heart-warming as the opportunity for the two worst teams in world football to face each other was, regrettably it would be something of a practical impossibility for such a match to occur regularly. So no return match would ever happen, and for the time being, such a clash of the worst of the worst has yet to be repeated.

Having proven themselves to be the undisputed worst team in the world, it would be nearly two years before Montserrat would take to the field as a national team again, this time in the first qualifying round for the 2006 World Cup. Fortunes hadn't changed for the better sadly though, as dreams of making it all the way to Germany didn't last much longer than the fifteen minutes it took Bermuda to score the opening goal of what would prove to be a 13-0 defeat in their preliminary round first leg. The home leg was a relative success as Montserrat succumbed to a mere 7-0 defeat in front of just two hundred and fifty optimistic souls. It would continue in this vein for years to come. Montserrat would spend nigh on a decade at the foot of the rankings.

Worst in the World

Chapter 3: David and Goliath

All appeared equal as the two lines of eleven men stood among the manicured lawns and gently swaying palm trees. They stood mostly in silent contemplation, save for one or two offering up the occasional verbal encouragement to their teammates, as they waited to march on to the carpet-like grass of the luxurious resort's sports facilities. Eleven men in blue and eleven men in white, about to do battle in front of a smattering of noisy fans up in the tropical scenic rolling hills of central Guam. But things were far from equal. Guam's players, the erstwhile men in blue, were representing their small dot of an island in the western Pacific Ocean with a population of a little over 160,000. The visitors were the cream of the footballing crop of the relative giant of Mongolia, a nation of more than three million, and one ranked comfortably higher than last-placed Guam.

If that weren't enough of a disparity, add in the fact that Guam's tiny land mass could fit into Mongolia almost three hundred times over and it is clear that equality was not the order of the day. For Guam, Mongolia were the Goliath to their David, the giant to their dwarf, the shark to their minnow. But football can be a great leveller. For all the differences in population and player-base, it still comes down, as it always does, to eleven versus eleven.

Lining up for Guam that day in April 2009 in an East Asian Championship first round group stage match was a very youthful squad made up of a smattering of semi-professional players plus one or two students. Several teenagers, including a confident looking nineteen-year-old striker, Christopher Mendiola, were part of the team. Such was the paucity of the playing pool available to Guam – around six hundred registered players – that this was already Mendiola's third season playing for his national team, making him one of the more seasoned regulars despite his lack of years.

Slightly older, but with a similar level of experience was the man who would look to provide Mendiola's supply line in attack, the Sheringham to Mendiola's Shearer, Jason Cunliffe. Towering over them all was the goalkeeper, Brett Maluwelmeng, a chunky imposing giant of a man making only his third appearance for the national team. He was one of a handful of US-born players in the squad, who in addition to a few islanders based in America and playing in American lower leagues or colleges, had returned to Guam to add a little football-savvy to go with the local enthusiasm. Their Japanese coach, Norio Tsukitate, was sanguine ahead of the challenge: 'Even if we can't build on our ability we want to be a team that makes up for it with feeling.'[32]

For the worst teams in the world, more often than not lacking in most of the requisite resources – population, registered players, facilities, funding – taking on a relative giant is a fairly regular occurrence. Sometimes they take on the true giants of the game – think San Marino's efforts in succumbing to Germany – and naturally on those occasions the best they can hope for is to limit the damage rather than forlornly striving for an unobtainable victory. But for the lowliest teams of them all, giant killing can be a flexible concept. On the rare occasions that a member of the worst in the world club causes an upset and wins, it is often at the expense of someone equally small. Sometimes, though, it is at the expense of someone larger, by one measure or another. The occasional slaying of a relative giant is the stuff of dreams for the worst teams in the world.

When talking about two nations who count their populations in the thousands rather than the millions, taking on an opponent whose population is several times your own is no small task. Montserrat's long stint as the worst team in world football came to an astonishing end during the 2012 Caribbean Cup, of which more later in the book, against the British Virgin Islands. That may sound like the very definition of two miniscule oceanic specks clashing in a contest of questionable quality, but in its own way it was a clash between little and large. Sparsely populated its islands may be, but the British Virgin Islands boasts a population of almost 24,000, roughly four times the size of Montserrat. This is indeed small fry, but when dealing in such diminutive numbers the difference is all the more crucial.

With the extra weight of numbers behind them, the British Virgin Islands have traditionally had the upper hand over Montserrat, winning all of their previous meetings, and comfortably so. But on this hot and steamy day in September 2012, Montserrat registered a stunning 7-0 victory over their Caribbean counterparts.

Taking things up a notch or two with a swift switch to the South Pacific, the Cook Islands found themselves stranded at the foot of the rankings in 2009. A friendly double-header against Tonga saw them claw their way slightly higher up the table with a draw and a win in the two matches. Nothing particularly remarkable about that you might imagine, other than the fact that Tonga's population is roughly ten times the size that of the Cook Islands' mere 11,000.

And yet those two examples of the worst in the world punching well above their weight pale into insignificance when looking once more at the original last placed team in FIFA's rankings: Macau. Their long-standing spell at the bottom in the early years of football's meritocracy came to an abrupt end with an impressive 5-1 win over the Philippines. Macau is not of the mini-magnitude of Montserrat or the Cook Islands in terms of population. Far from it in fact. At over 600,000 it is a crowded, cluttered, city-state. Squeezed into an area little over 31km^2 Macau can lay claim to being the most densely populated region in the world. But the Philippines are another beast altogether. With a population nearing 100 million it is over one hundred and sixty times the size of the Chinese Special Administrative Region that so resoundingly beat them in this match in 1996.

It wasn't even as though the Philippines had the excuse of little footballing tradition to fall back on either. As a Spanish colonial outpost, it became one of Asia's earliest practitioners of football in the first half of the twentieth century and accordingly they were one of Asia's strongest. Times have changed clearly, and Macau's impressive win was achieved with what was by far the biggest magnitude of population differential that a worst in the world team has ever managed.

* * * * *

Guam's footballing past is a far from salubrious one. As mentioned in the opening chapter, they were once holders of the record for the heaviest defeat in international football, losing 19-0 to Iran in qualification for the 2002 World Cup. This horrendous defeat saw the tiny Pacific territory fall even lower than the 200th place they held at the time to reach the bottom of the world rankings a couple of years later. This steady, inexorable descent culminated in a 6-0 defeat by fellow basement dwellers Bhutan in the qualifying rounds of the

2004 Asian Cup. It may not have been such a resounding score line but the limited nature of the opposition meant that it had the biggest demoralising effect. As with Bhutan's win over Montserrat in the previous chapter, being comprehensively beaten by one of the weakest of the weak is a particularly humiliating experience, and it was one which ushered in an era of many more heavy beatings. Hong Kong twice racked up fifteen goals against Guam, while North Korea took things to another level with a 21-0 win in the 2005 East Asian Championship.

Having joined FIFA in 1996 this Pacific island nation, like American Samoa an unincorporated territory of the United States, played their first officially sanctioned matches in that year's Asian Cup qualifying group. Any thoughts of a gentle introduction to world football were swiftly cast aside when their opponent for their opening clash was announced. Standing in their way were the Asian superpower of South Korea, regular World Cup finalists and always one of the strongest in the region.

Perhaps fortunately it wasn't a full strength Korean team that took part in the qualifying group, but it was more than enough to dispatch Guam with minimum fuss. It could easily have been more than the 9-0 it ended, but Guam would at least have the minor consolation of not conceding double figures. Another 9-0 defeat followed against Vietnam in their next game before the final match with Chinese Taipei brought another nine goals in Guam's net – their defence were nothing if not consistent – but it also saw a magnificent two goals scored; Guam's first official international goals.

Not only that, but one of those who scored was a young man named Ryan Stepp, who was just fifteen-years-old at the time, making him one of the youngest international goal scorers ever. According to the statistical website the Recreational Sport Soccer Statistics Foundation,[33] at the time of his goal he was the fourth youngest international goal scorer of all time. A magnificent achievement for such a young man of course, but it embodied the limited playing resources at Guam's disposal that a fifteen-year-old was in such a match in the first place. Remarkable feat or not, it still meant three defeats from three for Guam on their international debut, conceding nine of each occasion, and with it a place at the bottom of the world.

44

But if that inauspicious opening was a tough baptism, 2002 would be their real low point. Not only was Guam's first World Cup campaign a record-breaking disappointment, but that year they also contrived to concede nineteen goals to China in an Asian Cup qualifier. Not that it was all bad news. The frequent beatings were interspersed with one or two standout victories against those even smaller and weaker. Sadly, the only opponents they beat, their neighbours to the north, the Northern Mariana Islands, and the island of Pohnpei – a part of the Federated States of Micronesia – weren't recognised FIFA nations. Naturally then, those victories were a wasted effort as far as the rankings were concerned, having no bearing on Guam's standing. Worse still, they were the only two victories Guam had managed since becoming FIFA members in 1996 adding to the frustration that they made no difference to Guam's worst in the world tag. Every other match they had played, they had lost, many of them by double figures.

Guam and Mongolia had faced each other a handful of times in the not too distant past in previous opening rounds of the East Asian Championship. The tournament caters for a subset of the Asian Confederation and includes the real giants of Japan, South Korea and China in its latter stages as well as the likes of Mongolia, Macau, Hong Kong and Guam's island neighbours from the Northern Mariana Islands in the preliminary rounds. On each occasion they'd previously met, it was Mongolia who had emerged victorious: 2-0 in 2003, 4-1 in 2005 and 5-2 in 2007. For Guam, these progressively heavier defeats had actually been something of a high point, surrounded as they were by altogether more humbling defeats to the likes of Hong Kong, Chinese Taipei and the previously mentioned resounding thrashing from North Korea in the 2005 East Asian Championship. But defeat is defeat, and Mongolia had inflicted plenty of them on Guam in their past meetings.

* * * * *

The Leo Palace Resort in Guam is more used to welcoming holidaymakers and businessmen to its luxurious and lush surroundings than it is to hosting international football. Hidden amongst the swanky environs of expansive and expensive condominiums, pristine golf courses, and numerous heated pools, are one or two high-end sports facilities. These have played host to professional golf tournaments, baseball camps, and the occasional visit from a Japanese or Korean top flight football team on a pre-season tour.

Described on *Visit Guam*'s website as a "Paradise City that awaits you in the hills" it is an unlikely setting for an international football tournament. And yet the national teams of Mongolia, Macau and the Northern Mariana Islands had joined that of the hosts in taking up residence in the exclusive resort to compete for the right to progress to the semi-final round and the chance to take on some slightly bigger fish.

The warm sunshine of Guam was quite a shock to the system for the Mongolians. More accustomed to temperatures in Ulaanbaatar pushing the mercury well below freezing at that time of year, the players would have to endure a temperature difference of nearing forty degrees to play in the tropical heat. 'We can't play outdoors in Mongolia right now,' the Mongolian head coach Ishdorj Otgonbayar noted ahead of the tournament. 'The snow will melt in July.'[34] Needless to say, in such bitter conditions their pre-tournament training had taken place indoors, save for a late-winter outdoor training camp in snow-laden surroundings aimed at toughening the players up.

Perhaps unsurprisingly, given their opponent's snow-hampered preparations, the match began with Guam's young bucks to the fore and on the offensive, buoyed on by their boisterous, if numerically limited, following. As early as the ninth minute of play, Christopher Mendiola combined with Jason Cunliffe with a neat, crisp one-two before firing into the net from just inside the penalty area. If six hundred fans can be said to cause bedlam, then that is what happened as the happy hundreds watching celebrated an infrequently experienced lead. They had been there before however. Two years before, in losing 5-2 to Mongolia, Guam had even led 2-0 before succumbing to five Mongolian strikes. This time, the determination was to achieve a different outcome for a change.

The Mongolian response was swift. From the restart, a foray into the Guam half saw a speculative effort sent goal-ward by the defender Tserenjav Enkhjargal from all of thirty yards out. It smacked off the crossbar with a thud, to the audible relief of the Guamanian contingent. That let-off spurred Guam forwards once more and for the remainder of the first half it was they who made the running again. Cunliffe and Mendiola both had their chances to increase the lead, but by half-time the slender one goal advantage remained.

Things would be different after the break however. In spite of their poor first half, Mongolia were the higher rated team and they set about demonstrating why with a level of intensity that Guam had never before been able to contain. In the Guam goal, big Brett Maluwelmeng was kept busy as the chances rained in. His teammates, lacking the wherewithal to keep any sustained possession of the ball as the rejuvenated Mongolians poured forwards, now chased shadows in an effort to contain as best they could. Momentum had irrevocably shifted. Chance after chance came Mongolia's way as the earlier scoring opportunities for the men in blue faded further from recollection.

Under such attrition, Guam had repeatedly floundered in the past. All prior attempts to stem a relentless opposing tide had resulted in defences breached and goalkeeper beaten, time and time again. But it was to be different this day. Brett Maluwelmeng would not concede and allow the precious lead to slip. Rather, he played the game of his life, turning away all the Mongolians could throw at him. Their stretched, strained and sliced defence would not be breached.

The closest Mongolia came was from a late free-kick from the edge of the box, fired in left-footed and seemingly heading for the corner of the goal. A leaping Maluwelmeng palmed it away one-handed to safety, the lead remaining safely intact. In the closing minutes, the Mongolian invasion continued while Maluwelmeng, ably assisted by those scurrying around chasing down their opponents ahead of him, turned each effort away. The excitable home crowd counted down the final seconds in a crescendo of ever-increasing volume, before the grandest cheer of them all as the Korean referee signalled an end to the match. Mongolia's knack for regularly beating their Guamanian opponents in this tournament had at last been overcome. The whistle was met with a mixture of joy and relief by those involved; thirteen years of hurt since joining FIFA was finally, gloriously, conclusively over.

'We finally got a win,' was the rather neat summation of Guam's coach Tsukitate, himself having endured five years at the helm, searching, striving, straining for that elusive first official victory. 'We had something to prove today, and I think we did,'[35] he added with pride. Those thirteen years since achieving FIFA recognition had brought nothing but defeat against other FIFA nations. And what is more, since the founding of Guam's Football Association in 1975, it was their first victory against a FIFA-affiliated nation. A thirty-four year quest was at an end. For it all to end so heroically against the strongest-rated team in this particular tournament was the stuff of dreams. Mongolia are no world-beaters, far from it, but this was no sneaky win over an equally small rival. Guam had slain their giant.

'The result is due to all the hard work everyone has continuously been putting in,' continued Tsukitate. 'It's a big victory for us, especially considering that situation was something new for us. The team has grown a lot to be able to win by a goal.'[36] The rarity of protecting a lead late in a game was something only previously experienced in the occasional close encounter with the Northern Mariana Islands. This was altogether grander, altogether more meaningful, and all the sweeter for it. 'I thought we had to score more goals after the first one because Mongolia is a tough team,' was the goal-scoring hero Mendiola's post-match verdict.[37]

Guam followed this historic win by beating their near neighbours from Northern Mariana 2-1 before facing a tournament decider against Macau. With Mongolia having reasserted their authority by winning both of their remaining games, Guam only required a draw to ensure top spot in the group and with it an unprecedented place in the next round of the East Asian Championship. Trailing 2-1 as the game neared its conclusion it appeared that for all their exploits, Guam were to miss out on qualification at the very last. They had come such a long way, made such strides, that to miss out at this late stage shouldn't have been such a disappointing prospect, but there was no escaping that it would be.

As the match entered stoppage time, a surge forward from Guam defender Scott Gurrero, playing as an emergency forward in the latter stages as desperation increased, saw him slip the ball through to Jason Cunliffe. He coolly slotted the ball past the onrushing Macau goalkeeper for a dramatic and decisive equaliser. A previously unthinkable draw left Guam in uncharted territory. In the space of a few short days, they'd racked up their first official win and then, after the victory over their unranked neighbours, followed it up with their

48

first official draw to top the group and progress to the next round for the first time.

'We can only go up from here,' was Cunliffe's assessment.[38] Guam's ranking, after this successful week in the sun, would at least for now be headed that way.

Worst in the World

Chapter 4: Giant Strides

'There is no point in punching someone who is thirty-six positions below us,' declared Sri Lanka's former national team captain Ashok Nawgalage. 'Playing Bhutan is not very useful, even in terms of acquiring experience.'[39] Call it complacent, call it condescending, call it belittling, call it what you will. The pointlessness and futility of facing the worst team in the world is an attitude that has been shared by many a player, coach and pundit before this ominous statement from the former Sri Lanka player. A meaningless exercise, a hiding to nothing. Little more than an obligation that the stronger team must endure before moving on to the real, challenging matches further ahead.

'There is no need to worry about past results and the world ranking does not matter. It is just a number,' countered Bhutan's twenty-four-year-old captain, the presciently named Karma Shedrup Tshering, defiantly ahead of his country's first ever World Cup qualifying match. 'It is not a reflection of our performance, but the frequency of matches that we have played.'[40] With a mostly amateur team and little funding, players' and officials' priorities often lie outside international football. Tshering, for instance, is a pilot with the national airline when he's not captaining the national team.

The last full international Bhutan had played was a 5-2 defeat to Sri Lanka eighteen months earlier in the South Asian Football Federation Championship of 2013. And now, some 242 days after Germany hoisted the glittering World Cup prize aloft in Rio de Janeiro in 2014, Bhutan found themselves as one of a handful of the world's weakest teams who opened the qualifying competition for the 2018 edition in Asia's opening round. Their opponents were Sri Lanka once more, who sat comfortably higher than Bhutan in the world rankings and who had beaten them on all five occasions the teams had met. To add to the contrast, Sri Lanka could draw on the best of a population of over twenty million, compared to Bhutan's comparatively paltry eight-hundred thousand.

Bhutan had finally sunk to the bottom of FIFA's rankings in July 2012, their resounding win over Montserrat now nothing but a distant, pleasant memory. They had remained stranded there for almost three years, having lost every match they'd played since 2008.

That losing run now stood at nineteen games and ahead of a first ever World Cup qualification appearance, there was little evidence to counter the condescension of the Sri Lankans. With a young squad made up almost entirely of students – some at college, others still in high school – and part-time players, one as young as sixteen, they played for the love of the game, a hobby that had taken them to the World Cup qualifiers. As such, they were surely ripe for plucking by Sri Lanka's eminently more experienced, able and battle-hardened squad.

Although eligible to have entered every World Cup from the 2006 tournament onwards, Bhutan had previously floundered at the application stage, finding neither the will nor the money required to finance a qualifying campaign when it came time for the entries to be submitted to FIFA. They did make it as far as entering the 2010 World Cup before withdrawing because their stadium, still the picturesque Changlimithang Stadium where Montserrat were beaten in 2002, would not be upgraded (as demanded by FIFA) in time. But more usually it was for financial reasons that Bhutan stayed holed up in their Himalayan Kingdom whenever the World Cup qualifiers rolled around; a sports-related return to their old isolationist ways.

This time around, FIFA's not inconsiderable funds had come to the aid of the Bhutanese, with financial assistance providing the means, finally, for a first venture into the grandest tournament of them all. 'We couldn't participate in the World Cup qualifiers before because of the budget issues,' confirmed the head of Bhutan's Football Federation, and head of the sporting purse-strings Ugen Tsechup Dorji.[41] Sitting out previous World Cups had seemed the only natural thing to do. Was there any need to waste vital funds on a likely short-lived and potentially humiliating World Cup when there were far more pressing needs at home? This is a view understandably held by more than one footballing minnow. Limited budgets would be better spent developing youth programs or upgrading ramshackle facilities than sending a team overseas as perennial lambs to the slaughter.

Bhutan had since become GOAL programme beneficiaries, with vast improvements made to a number of facilities on the back of the FIFA dime. Initially paying for an improved youth set-up over recent years, these various funding initiatives had eventually culminated in improved facilities to benefit the senior squad in 2014. Sepp Blatter himself visited Thimphu to open the new training complex adjacent to the national stadium, complete with year-round artificial pitches and floodlights. The main stadium's pitch was improved too: the patchy, puddle-strewn quagmire of years before now gone, replaced with a hybrid 3G pitch. Training programmes to improve coaching standards were implemented and there was an increased focus on youth training and grassroots football. The future was in hand then, but what of the present national team? With all of these FIFA-funded initiatives in place, the governing body's ambition of full international participation was always likely to see Bhutan finally making their World Cup bow in the 2018 qualifiers.

A further incentive came in the form of a "special additional support" grant of US$300,000 to any member participating in the initial preliminary stages. With costs covered, there was no longer any avoiding the big tournament. Therefore, as the preliminary tie with Sri Lanka approached, efforts were made to raise the level of the senior team in the limited time available. The dangling carrot to all taking part at this early stage – the twelve lowest ranked of Asia's forty-six teams – was the prospect of eight guaranteed group matches in the next round, including taking on one of the region's strongest. The victor in this Sri Lanka-Bhutan tie could soon find themselves in a group alongside Japan, South Korea or Australia. To Bhutan, this prospect would be akin to qualifying for the World Cup, such would be the step up in quality and profile.

With the dual challenges of lack of experience and the prospect of travelling to face Sri Lanka in the stifling heat of coastal Colombo for the first leg, Bhutan's newly acquired funds were put to use in various ways. A select group of the eighteen-man national squad would be paid a monthly salary of 10,000 ngultrum, a shade over £100, in an effort to allow them to train together with sufficient regularity in the weeks prior to the matches. In a team containing one lone professional player, the teenage striker Chencho Gyeltshen who plays in the Thai League and is known somewhat optimistically as "the Ronaldo of Bhutan", this allowed a level of preparation that was hitherto unknown in Bhutanese football.

The team also spent a week training in Thailand prior to travelling on to Colombo for the first leg in an effort to acclimatise and adapt to the unfamiliar hot conditions. They trained daily in temperatures approaching thirty-eight degrees. 'Usually you need about two weeks, but we tried to use the one week we had in Thailand in an efficient way to adapt to the conditions,' said the national team coach Chokey Nima.[42] In their favour was the prospect of Sri Lanka feeling equally out of their comfort zone once they reached the return leg in Thimphu's high altitude; an equally unsettling prospect.

Like his captain, Ugen Dorji declared himself 'not really bothered' by the title of the world's worst team and was 'hopeful' ahead of the Sri Lankan matches. 'Sri Lanka is a team that is not way, way beyond the quality level of football that is being played in Bhutan. It would depend on that particular day, how our boys perform.'[43]

* * * * *

On the shores of the Indian Ocean, Sri Lanka's palm-fringed capital, Colombo, was a sultry, sweltering, sticky thirty-five degrees on this balmy Thursday afternoon. The Sugathadasa Stadium, a small, compact stadium with low-lying stands circling an athletics track in a leafy, tree-lined area of the city is little more than a long clearance away from Colombo's busy harbour, and the ocean beyond. The Bhutanese team had arrived in Colombo at two in the morning a couple of days before the match after their jaunt to Thailand and were looking forward to their first taste of World Cup action.

Sri Lanka's team were equally as confident as their former captain, he of the condescension. 'All countries dream of the World Cup,' commented the striker Sanjeev Shanmugarajah. 'We are planning a 4-0 score.' The current captain was equally bullish, stating 'We are going for the kill.' The coach might be expected to be rather more level-headed, not wishing to tempt fate or provide ammunition for the opposition, but alas no. 'We can make our dream come true,' was the rallying cry from Sri Lanka's much-travelled Serbian coach Nikola Kavazovic.[44]

A police escort accompanied Bhutan's team as their coach made its way through the heavy Colombo traffic to the stadium. The population of Colombo were clearly more concerned with going about their daily business than witnessing the World Cup kick off as the stands remained almost empty, bereft of support for the confident home team. In amongst the few thousand who had turned out, a sizeable minority clustered in the main stand were supporting the visitors; a group of Bhutanese medical students who lived in Colombo.

Despite the oppressive conditions, the men from the mountains attacked from the off in the early stages belying their lowly status. Chances came along regularly in the opening exchanges with Chencho Gyeltshen hitting the post with an early effort before Karma Tshering missed an easy opportunity to give his side the lead. If these opportunities made it clear that the anticipated comfortable Sri Lankan victory was not to be, they didn't tell the whole story. Vastly improved they may have been, but Bhutan were still facing a higher rated opponent. As if to emphasise this point, Sri Lanka came very close themselves with a fierce, fizzing shot which thumped off the cross-bar and away. After this venture forward, the host's attacks gradually became more frequent, as Bhutan settled into a diligent defensive attitude combined with some fast counter-attacking football.

The match remained scoreless as the minutes dwindled away. Only six were remaining when, after a period of sustained Sri Lankan pressure, a Bhutan break saw Gyeltshen marauding down the right wing, and tricking his way past the Sri Lankan full back. He burst into the box, drawing the keeper towards him as he reached the bye-line. He cut the ball back for the twenty-one year-old midfielder Tshering Dorji who was rushing into the goalmouth in support. Dorji took a touch to control the ball before calmly and gleefully firing past the backpedalling, scrambling defenders attempting to cover for their now absent goalkeeper. Goal! The Bhutanese players, stunned by this turn of events, flocked after Dorji as he ran towards the bench in wild celebration. The happy few Bhutan fans in the stands made a delirious din and hailed their compatriots' first World Cup goal.

The equally stunned Sri Lankans were unable to respond in the remaining minutes, leaving the worst team in international football to win their first ever World Cup match 1-0. 'It's a very happy moment for my life,' reflected the jubilant goal scorer afterwards. 'It was a moment that I have been waiting for; it was a precious moment to score.'[45]

Suddenly headlines and reports were popping up on websites all over the world hailing the unexpected victory with their focus firmly trained on the worst in the world tag: "A Moment Atop the World for Bhutan's Last-Ranked Team" in the *New York Times*, "World's Worst team Bhutan kick off 2018 World Cup qualifying with victory" in the *Guardian*, "World's Worst Football Team Bhutan Play First World Cup Game…and Win" in the *Bleacher Report*, "Bhutan…take giant killing strides in World Cup qualifiers" in *Inside World Football*. It's hard to imagine that so much attention had ever been given to so lowly a preliminary match before. FIFA President Sepp Blatter even got in on the act, describing the result as 'a wonderful, historic moment' on Twitter.

The vanquished Sri Lankan coach sat in the post-match news conference, still with an air of defiance and optimism but an acceptance of the complacency that seemed to have pervaded his team. 'Yes, it is embarrassing, losing to the worst team in the world,' he said. 'They were a better team and they deserve to win. We thought the Bhutan team [were] going to be easy but things were totally different on the field. But I expect we will win the second game. And if I don't, I will have an unexpected holiday for a few months.'[46]

Having failed to beat Bhutan in the heat of Colombo, Sri Lanka's task had surely become exponentially more awkward by having to overcome this deficit in the altitude of Thimphu. As Karma Tshering noted to a *New York Times* journalist after the match, 'it will be freezing' and up to 30,000 fans were expected to attend the second leg, providing a strong visible and vocal support.

'We will celebrate today, but we are also preparing for the next challenge,' Bhutan coach Nima told the press.[47] The manner of that celebration was slightly unorthodox, as the victorious players hailed this opening win with a visit to the KFC next door to their Colombo hotel. The following morning the team travelled home to be met at the airport by a group of their supporters carrying large banners hailing the team's first leg win. While the majority of the team would begin preparations for the crucial second match, their captain Tshering had other business to attend to, flying to Singapore and back as a pilot with the national carrier. The worst in the world tag was assured to be expunged come the next world rankings, but now the Bhutan team had the chance to achieve something more, something truly magnificent.

'Nobody in Bhutan expected us to win,' Tshering told the *Guardian* ahead of the second match. 'We have been all over the news and it is a pretty historic moment. All the talk when we play international matches is always about how many we're going to concede or just hoping to keep the score line low. But we didn't concede and, even better, we won – so everyone was very surprised and shocked about it.'

'Everyone was talking about us being at the bottom but we didn't feel any pressure because you can only go one way from there, and that's upwards,' he added. 'All the expectation was on Sri Lanka and they were talking a lot about beating us, but we kept our calm and let our football talk for us.'[48]

Unexpectedly within touching distance of the group stages, the weight of newfound expectation bearing down on the players and their young captain was gaining in intensity. The world's attention was now focused on their exploits from afar. And yet there was still the nagging feeling that Sri Lanka were far from done. Complacency had cost them in the first match, and would surely not be an issue again. Sri Lanka would be desperate to turn the tie around and justify their billing as favourites. Bhutan had to be wary. Much had been achieved - now it was time to complete the task.

'The job is only half done and we still have a game to go,' added Tshering. 'We are trying to keep the players calm and reduce any pressure, which will be greater because we are playing at home and expecting huge support. There is going to be a lot of pressure on the players for this one – and especially for me as team captain.' Chokey Nima accepted that the odds were still against his team. 'But we are going to win,' he added with a smile.[49]

* * * * *

If the increased pressure was getting to Karma Tshering and his teammates, it wasn't showing. A couple of hours ahead of the crucial second leg, the players had visited a monastery high up in the green-covered mountains surrounding Thimphu for a blessing and a spiritual consultation. The blessing was straightforward enough, administered by an orange-robed monk amidst the serenity of the quiet, contemplative location. The consultation on the other hand was not given by the monk, nor was it by the team's coach. It was a consultation with some dice, or *mo*.

In Buddhist tradition, people are known to consult the *mo* when making important decisions relating to health, work, and travel in particular, in a more theological version of a magic eight-ball. There are various, complex interpretations of what the resulting dice throws mean, but the answers are said to come from Manjushri, the Bodhisattva of wisdom. On the issue of international football success, it seems, even numbers were bad luck, and odd were good.

'I threw three threes,' said Tshering to an accompanying *New York Times* journalist. 'I think it was a good throw.'[50]

At the same time as the *mo* were being consulted high above Thimphu, in the Changlimithang Stadium the crowds were flocking into the stands in huge numbers from as early as four hours ahead of kick off. Many were wearing national dress, but with additional smatterings of orange and yellow, the national colours. Entry was free to those who could get in, though thousands more were locked outside. In what was an early evening kick off, many workers had been sent home early, the government declaring a half-day holiday for state employees, so they could either get to the stadium or watch the match on the national broadcaster's wall-to-wall coverage. The conditions couldn't have been more different from those in Colombo a few days earlier. Hot and humid had been replaced with cold and breezy, with the added impact of high altitude.

Amidst the chaotic din, Bhutan got off to a dream start when a long ball upfield, in only the fifth minute, fell to the team's lone professional player, eighteen-year-old Chencho Gyeltshen. He beat the onrushing Sri Lankan keeper to the ball and delicately flicked it over him and into the net from an acutely narrow angle. The noise lifted a few decibels higher as the huge crowd now anticipated a comfortable win. But Sri Lanka levelled things shortly before half time when a weak header from a corner somehow snuck past both the diving Bhutanese goalkeeper, Hari Gurung, and the defender guarding the post behind him. This led to a rather nervy and more open second half. As it stood, Sri Lanka were just a goal away from winning the tie on away goals.

The action flowed one way then the other as chances came and went at both ends. By the 87th minute, there had been no additional scoring, but the tension had become almost unbearable for those watching. Each Sri Lankan attack, and there were many, was met with anguished screams and wails from the thousands watching as the increasingly desperate visitors surged forwards in search of the clinching goal. Amidst the apprehension, a lofted cross beyond Bhutan's far post was headed back across goal by a Sri Lankan forward. The Bhutanese goalkeeper Gurung had been drawn to the cross like a moth to a flame, and as the ball was centred once more to the poised Sri Lankan striker he was out of position. With the goal gaping, the net seemed destined to bulge but Gurung, in a desperate, all-or-nothing scramble, flung himself at it and pushed the ball towards the post. The crowd's earlier anguished screams were now replaced momentarily by a stunned silence as the ball bounced off the upright. It could just as easily have bounced into the goal as out, but luck, or perhaps the roll of the dice, was on Bhutan's side. The ball was cleared by the defence, away to safety; the slender width of the post the difference between aggregate victory and defeat.

Two minutes later as the clock ticked on to the ninety-minute mark, a long cross-field pass found Gyeltshen once more, deep inside the Sri Lankan half. He zigzagged through the box, dancing past three exhausted defenders before firing low under the keeper to score a dramatic late winner. Pandemonium once more in the stands and on the pitch as Gyeltshen disappeared under a pile of jubilant teammates. The Bhutanese match commentator, unused to such sporting drama, struggled to keep a sense of perspective, hailing: "It might still be early to say so, but Bhutan is on the road to Russia!" His giddy co-commentator got in on the act too: "That might just be the most crucial goal that he will ever score in his career. That might be the goal that," he paused, as if judging whether he should really say it or not, before adding the coup de grace: "…takes us to the World Cup!"

Where previously there had been silence there was now unbridled joy as the stadium, player and spectator alike, erupted. All except the Sri Lankans of course, many of whom slumped to their knees on the turf as defeat was now assured, and their World Cup hopes extinguished. Gyeltshen, a stylish player and stylish young man with elegant and slickly coiffured hair and chiselled jaw, had, with that strike of his boot, sealed his place as a national superstar. "A new hero is born today here," was one of the commentator's more accurate statements in the aftermath of Gyeltshen's goal. The man himself re-emerged from under his teammates with a severe limp, and had to be substituted before the match could restart for the closing few moments.

The final whistle, a minute or so later, confirmed a repeat giant killing triumph, the whistle acting like an energy boost to the Bhutanese players who sprinted off in all directions in delirious delight. In the stands, strangers hugged each other and flags were waved enthusiastically all around. The players swiftly recovered their composure and went across to shake the hands of their beaten counterparts. They then linked arms and bowed to the packed stands, thankful for their support and accepting the adoring crowd's acclaim. "They are our Neil Armstrong," added the commentator with a final dramatic flourish. "Our first men on the moon."

'We had so many chances, but had one good play and scored the second,' Tshering said in the glow of victory. 'We let them hear the roar of the Dragon.'[51] The crowd too made their roar heard. Joyous supporters banged drums and chanted, "Now we're not the worst team!" after their heroes saw out the win, before heading into the Thimphu streets for an impromptu party.

For national team coach Chokey Nima, the victories were particularly significant, wiping away old wounds. He had been in the Bhutan team that suffered the 20-0 demolition by Kuwait in 2000. Afflicted by the past he may have been, but his young squad were unburdened by those memories. 'Most of our players were hardly old enough to walk or talk when it happened,' explained Tshering. 'None of us have watched it, so things like that don't have a psychological effect on us.'[52]

Bhutan would now go on to the group stages of Asian qualifying, where the real giants of the region lay in wait. Heavy defeats would undoubtedly follow, but for the cash-strapped Bhutan Football Federation, the eight-match guarantee of the group stages promised to be a financial windfall, ensuring ongoing support for their development initiatives. It would also bring an unprecedented level of play and intensity for Tshering and Bhutan to cope with, but would provide a regularity of matches unlike anything the team had ever known. 'Maybe we would like to play Japan now,' Nima joked in the aftermath of victory.[53] Having stepped away from the foot of the rankings, after a few years firmly rooted to the bottom, those matches would provide the real test of just how far Bhutan had come.

Worst in the World

Chapter 5: New Arrivals

'We cannot see our first win coming in the next few years but we will never quit,' said the coach of the East Timor national team, Pedro Almeida. 'We have no resources to keep this team together and we barely have grass to play on.'[54]

These bleak remarks came after Almeida's East Timor side had clocked up over two years stuck at the bottom of the world rankings with seemingly little hope of escape. Having joined FIFA in 2005, they played their first official matches the following year and promptly lost 5-0 twice within three days. Their place in the world order was set at dead last, and there it would remain as the new nation clocked up one defeat after another. Of all the countries who have become new members of FIFA since the rankings began, East Timor were one of the weakest, most under-resourced, and least equipped to make a rapid breakaway from the bottom of the rankings.

'The squad changes constantly because the players have families and cannot afford time off work,' continued Almeida. 'When they are twenty-one or twenty-two they have to quit.' Such financial realities of life in the far reaches of football take their toll on squads, making international management at this level something of a juggling act. The frequent and extensive turnover of players makes establishing any settled team style or squad harmony that much more difficult. When football doesn't pay, other priorities take precedence. Players on this lowly rung are sometimes too busy providing for their families to accept the call-up to play in a minor South-East Asian tournament.

A team made up of soldiers, shopkeepers, fishermen, port workers and students had to accept that this was the reality of life for many of them. Leaving a job when money is tight to merely play football, even if that is for your country, means there is no one left to work, no one putting food on the table. Even the coach had more than just the footballing string to his bow. He was better known in East Timor's capital city of Dili as being a motorbike mechanic.

The one professional player in their ranks was the captain Alfonso Esteves, a Portuguese of East Timor descent who accepted the call to represent his forebears' home. After a stint playing in the minor professional leagues of the United States he moved to New South Wales' Wollongong FC to allow him closer contact with East Timor.

Added to those hindrances for East Timor was the lack of even half-decent training facilities. Or even more fundamentally, the lack of much grass on their ramshackle, rock-strewn pitches, rendering them barely usable. 'There is a lot of talent there and a lot of passion but there are no fields to play the game,' Esteves explained. 'There is no regular league. Sometimes, they organise tournaments for clubs to come together but when the tournament is finished there's nothing. Sixty per cent of the population is under twenty-five but Timor has no jobs. The kids just spend the day hanging out doing nothing.'[55]

East Timor operates on a different barometer of success to much of the football world. While stronger nations measure their achievements (or lack thereof) in terms of silverware, teams such as East Timor have a far more straightforward goal - they simply want to win. Winning even once would be the stuff of dreams. When languishing in the football doldrums, hope can seem a long-abandoned ideal, repeatedly cast aside in the face of an endless string of defeats.

East Timor, or Timor-Leste as it is officially known in its colonial Portuguese tongue, is a relatively new country, having only achieved independence in 2002. Comprising two small islets and the eastern half of the island of Timor, which it shares with Indonesia, East Timor, is one of the poorest, most deprived countries in Asia. The majority of its population, a shade over one million, is concentrated in the capital city, Dili, but live in some of the most poverty-stricken circumstances in the region.

When its former Portuguese masters moved out in the mid-1970s, the neighbouring Indonesians seized the opportunity afforded them by the ensuing instability and invaded the eastern end of Timor. Their military success led to the onset of a violent, vicious, brutal occupation that would last until 1999. For twenty-four years, the Indonesian government would inflict extrajudicial executions, systematic torture, starvation, and increasingly frequent massacres on the people of East Timor. Amidst a raft of unnecessarily harsh and arbitrary rules enforced by the occupiers were such trivialities as owning a radio being a punishable crime. Likewise, speaking a language other than Indonesian would lead to imprisonment in horrific, unimaginable conditions.

Indonesia relinquished control of the territory in 1999 following a United Nations sponsored referendum of self-determination and three years later East Timor was officially recognised as the first newly independent sovereign state of the twenty-first century. An estimated 180,000 Timorese had lost their lives during the occupation, and much of the country's infrastructure was destroyed. If competitive football was little more than an afterthought in amongst the misery, the simple joys of playing the game on whatever patch of dirt was available was one of the strands that kept the Timorese people together and their hopes alive. As succinctly put in an article on the Asian news outlet *Asia Foundation*, 'If the Timorese find their spiritual salvation in the Catholic Church, they find their physical salvation in football.'[56]

'For hundreds of years now, football has been the most popular sport in our country' added the East Timor FA President Francisco Kalaudi in slight time-related exaggeration. 'This can be partly attributed to the influence of the Portuguese colonisers. Since our independence in 2002, we have continuously been pushing forward our development.'[57]

'Timor is a new country and it doesn't have infrastructure for anything,' Esteves explained. 'But when you travel through the country, soccer is ninety per cent of everything. All the kids love to play. They don't even need a field they just want to kick the ball around. You see kids everywhere using two rocks to make a goal. They just play for hours.'[58]

The *Asia Foundation* continued the theme: 'Football gives Timorese a national identity. Saying football is Timor's national sport is an understatement. You can see it played anywhere, anytime, in the hot midday sun and in the downpour of tropical showers, in the mist-covered mountains, on the white sand beaches. Though most games are battled out on rough gravel or rutted fields, with old sneakers and bare feet.'[59] This poverty of resources applied to the higher reaches of the sport in East Timor, just as it did to the lower echelons with little in the way of facilities for a national team to train and play on.

Since independence, there has been a steady trickle of overseas aid and investment finding its way to the country but in the midst of so many problems, understandably very little of that has been available to spend on sport. Years of neglect and ruin had left the nascent nation with football facilities in dire need of attention, but they did gain from some outside help. Shortly after independence, the country benefitted in the form of pitches intended for youth football granted to them by the United Nations. These came with the pronouncement from the UN that 'through football you will learn about leadership, strategy and teamwork, and these are the key skills in the development of a new nation.' No pressure then.

Additionally, like their fellow no-hopers in Montserrat and Bhutan, East Timor have been beneficiaries of FIFA's GOAL programme to upgrade their national team's facilities, though this took rather longer to come to fruition. Alfredo Esteves described the previous state of the national stadium and training grounds pitifully. 'There are two fields but our main stadium is unsafe, and the other is just dirt and rocks, so we can't play matches there,' he said. 'But FIFA have said they will help us out. They've promised to build a new pitch by the end of 2009.' That did eventually come to pass, and also led to the construction of the Timorese Football Association's headquarters in Dili, and also a football academy. Artificial pitches followed in spruced up training facilities allowing the national teams to train in surroundings befitting international footballers, rather than on the grassless, almost rubble-like, pitches they'd been used to.

In spite of, or perhaps because of, all their difficulties, the rare occasions when the team did come together was cause for celebration in itself. 'The first time East Timor was invited to play in a big tournament, [was] the 2004 South East Asian Championship in Malaysia,' recalled Esteves. 'It was not too good because we lost all the games, but we did a good job because we got a team together.'[60] Those early defeats came prior to their inclusion in FIFA, but once official recognition was achieved nothing really changed in terms of any slender shred of success. Defeat on the field of play was all the new nation knew, although over time the margin of those defeats gradually narrowed as the squad developed.

'Maybe it's difficult to understand, but when you are on the field representing your country, every single improvement makes you feel so good,' Esteves explained. 'The first game we ever played against the Philippines, we lost by seven goals. The next one we lost 1-0. Everyone was happy losing just 1-0.'[61] They were happy because it signified something. Choosing a positive outlook, it didn't mean a missed opportunity or a sense of frustration at losing narrowly. Rather, it signified the huge steps that had been taken by the fledgling nation. It represented a progression towards competitiveness, albeit in the small pond of East Timor's particular region. It meant that there was hope. Hope that sooner rather than later, they would experience something other than defeat.

They had come close before. Very close. In the Asian preliminary rounds for the 2010 World Cup, held in late 2007, East Timor were paired with Hong Kong in a two-legged playoff. Unable to play at home in Dili's dilapidated and decrepit stadium, they instead opted to play their 'home' leg in nearby Bali. Perhaps the Hong Kong players underestimated their lowly opponents. Perhaps they were simply enjoying a trip to a holiday island rather than to Timor. Or perhaps East Timor played above themselves, making things difficult for Hong Kong. Whatever it was, the match was a close one. Fighting back from an early deficit, East Timor scored two of their own through Emilio da Silva, a twenty-five year-old striker who would go on to become both the country's top goal scorer and appearance holder. Sadly, his goals weren't enough to avoid defeat, with Hong Kong edging to a 3-2 win, but there could be no doubting the progress that this narrow loss signified.

Even more maddeningly, one of the three goals conceded was a self-inflicted wound. A clumsy, scuffed disaster of an own goal denied them a shock draw on their World Cup debut, with the captain Alfredo Esteves the man responsible, much to his own frustration and chagrin. Having run their more seasoned and experienced opponents so close in the first leg, redemption was not to be found in the return leg in Hong Kong. Their hosts finally showed their superiority in ruthless cold-blooded style, registering a resounding 8-1 win.

It would be another year before Esteves and his colleagues would play internationally again. Travelling to the Cambodian capital of Phnom Penh, East Timor took their place in the qualifying group of the South Asian Championships, the AFF Suzuki Cup as it was known at the time, alongside the other lower ranked teams of South East Asia. Opening with the aforementioned and, by Esteves at least, fondly recalled 1-0 loss to the Philippines, the next opponents were their hosts, Cambodia.

Phnom Penh's rather grandly and optimistically titled Olympic Stadium is a sterile, soulless concrete slab of a venue with a fading running track circling a patchwork pitch. Amongst its claims to fame, or rather infamy, the stadium was used as an execution site during the dark days of the Khmèr Rouge regime, where the leaders of the former Khmer Republic met their untimely and gruesome demise. On a more sporting theme, it was the setting for North Korea's qualification for their remarkably successful World Cup of 1966 in England, securing their place by beating Australia in a play off in front of a huge crowd.

With a capacity of around 50,000, the atmosphere could be intense when full. But on the day that Alfredo Esteves led out his East Timor teammates to face Cambodia in October 2008, the crumbling concrete stands were rather less packed. With just 12,000 people spread around the huge bowl-like stadium in the stiflingly claustrophobic afternoon heat, atmosphere was in short supply. Not that this worried the East Timor players. Buoyed by their earlier narrow loss to the Philippines, they set about the hosts in a diligent and positive manner. After Cambodia had failed to capitalise on the handful of chances they'd fashioned in the first half, a stunning strike from distance by East Timor's Anggisu Barbosa seconds before the interval opened the scoring.

If that weren't enough excitement for the Timor players to handle, they went two up midway through the second half when Jose Perreira picked himself up to convert a spot-kick having been fouled by the Cambodian keeper. Twenty minutes remained and East Timor's rag-tag band of footballers were within touching distance of a remarkable feat. Their first ever win was there for the taking. Twenty minutes to hold on, to survive, to endure.

On occasion, dreams do come true. More often, the dreamer awakes with a start to realise the dream was just that. Twenty minutes from success they may have been, but within the space of two minutes late in the game, the dream of victory was cruelly, callously, snatched away in a swift one-two. Cambodia converted a penalty kick of their own, moments before they grabbed a dramatic equaliser, leaving the Timorese facing the nightmare of potentially letting their best hope of victory slip agonisingly from their grasp. Barely a handful of minutes earlier, East Timor had been contemplating an unlikely victory, and yet now they were left clinging on to a draw, desperate and determined not to let their earlier enterprise go wholly unrewarded.

That they did indeed hold on to record their first ever draw, the first time they had not been beaten, could easily have felt like a loss. The circumstances, having led by two, could have meant the Timor players slouched off the pitch feeling downbeat, disappointed and ultimately unfulfilled. And yet it meant nothing of the sort to Alfredo Esteves and his fellow players. Rather, it meant a remarkable first draw, a signal that their progress was continuing, that the right path was being taken, that their hopes of inspiring their nation were nearing realisation. It also confirmed that they were no longer the world's whipping boys. A single draw it may have been, but it was a landmark achievement for the national side and heralded a climb up the rankings, at long last escaping the clutches of last place. Once more, the sporting press made use of the 'worst in the world' tag in headlines about this match, for instance *ESPN*'s "World's Worst Team Clinch First Ever Point."[62]

'Everyone was so delighted,' Esteves said afterwards. 'We know we are close [to winning]. The celebrations will be huge when we eventually win a match.'[63] His coach Pedro Almeida agreed: 'It was the first game we didn't lose. We're all very proud.' But he for one wouldn't be allowing his players to rest on their laurels. They may have escaped the worst in the world label, but having overseen this upturn in fortunes, Almeida wanted his players to continue improving. 'We are not happy with our world ranking and we are hoping our players will continue to improve.'[64] It wasn't a great leap forward, but it was a significant albeit small step in the right direction.

Their improvement wasn't enough to see them secure any wins or even another draw in their remaining two fixtures in Cambodia that autumn, but they had a newfound optimism. It was the kind of optimism that often abounds in new nations, as the pride of the newly independent can make the future glisten in the warm glow of anticipation. Such a feeling hadn't always been prevalent in East Timor, given its ongoing hardships, and had certainly been conspicuous by its absence from the national football team. 'It was a really big moment for everyone,' Esteves recalled. 'When we got the draw against Cambodia it was the cherry on the cake. We didn't think we would get a draw for a long time.'

'Timor is a small country that has never won anything, but we are getting closer,' added Esteves wistfully as he pictured his team's future. 'It will be a big celebration, maybe even around the world, when we do win a game. They have been suffering for many years with all the problems in the country. That first win will be something that will touch the world. It will be a great moment for everyone. It will be progress.'[65]

For now, the lone draw was sufficient to lift East Timor from world ranking ignominy to the lofty heights of 198th in the world; a precarious three places above the bottom. The ineptitude of others would keep them clear in the ensuing months and years ahead, though the search for that elusive first win would go on.

Indeed, it would be another four long years, and eight further defeats, in the wilderness before that win finally, gloriously came. When it did come, two factors were noticeably different from that first ever draw in 2008. Firstly, they weren't ranked as the worst in the world going into the match, albeit by a slender margin. And secondly, Alfredo Esteves would not be a part of it, having already retired from the game. His successors in the East Timor national team beat Cambodia, clearly their favourite opposition, in a resounding 5-1 victory in October 2012 to once and for all end their protracted winless run. Just like buses, having waited for so long for a win, another one came along just four days later as all thoughts of being perennial losers were finally banished. They had belatedly learned how to win, and had acquired the taste for it. There would be no looking back and no fear of sinking to the bottom of the rankings once more. Their ascent towards respectability had begun.

* * * * *

While a handful of weaker international debutants had a hard time climbing the rankings, East Timor, Guam, Montserrat and the likes, not all new nations necessarily suffered the same fate. Other new arrivals have had more success, some of them spending minimal time at the foot of the list before making good their escape, while others didn't even suffer that brief indignity, winning from the off and appearing higher up the list straight away, swiftly and efficiently leapfrogging those less fortunate and less capable.

Through the 1990s, many new nations emerged from the turmoil of Eastern Europe. As the old world order was split and destroyed, so a raft of independent countries took their places in the world's organisations. For many, membership of FIFA was almost as high on the list of priorities as gaining United Nations recognition. As the Soviet Union disintegrated and Yugoslavia more gradually splintered, the number of new national teams rapidly increased and they all took their place on the nascent world rankings.

For the stronger ones, the likes of Croatia, Slovenia, Ukraine, there was never any danger of hanging around in the depths of the rankings. Even amongst the weaker former Soviet 'stans', that batch of central Asian Republics, they mostly avoided the stigma of a brief stint at the bottom. Tajikistan, Kyrgyzstan, Kazakhstan and various other tongue twisters of a country all debuted on the rankings above last place. Less fortunate was the Caucasus republic of Azerbaijan, whose initial spell in FIFA resulted in a brief stint at the bottom, albeit for just two months.

Having won a string of unofficial matches following independence in 1991 whilst not yet affiliated to either UEFA or FIFA, Azerbaijan had to wait until 1994 to become members of both. Those earlier successes, against fellow former Soviets, meant nothing in terms of ranking points once Azerbaijan took their place in FIFA's meritocracy. Once FIFA membership was gained, Azerbaijan's first full international took place in April 1994 when they travelled to the less than mighty Malta to take on the hosts in a friendly. Surely, this was an easy opportunity to get off to a winning start and step quickly past the collection of lowly ranked nations? To say that things didn't get off to the most stellar of beginnings for the new nation would be something of an understatement.

Their small Mediterranean island opponents are not known for their football achievements but at the time they were ranked a startlingly high 82nd in the world, and made their superior experience tell. Before two minutes had ticked by, the Maltese had taken the lead. By half-time, it was 2-0, and three late goals piled on the Azeri misery to complete a 5-0 rout. A spot at the foot of the rankings was assured. It took a goalless draw with Turkey a few games and a few months later to finally rid them of that particular burden.

Much more recently, Montenegro's split from Serbia saw them taking their international football bow in 2007. Like Azerbaijan, they made the slightly premature mistake of winning prior to receiving FIFA recognition, in their case a 2-1 win over Hungary in front of their vocal home fans in Podgorica. But once membership of FIFA was confirmed, they travelled to Japan to play two friendlies and lost them both, to Japan and Colombia. Since these constituted their first official fixtures in FIFA's eyes, it was straight to the bottom of the rankings for the fledging nation. Home comforts proved more beneficial a few months down the line, when a draw was secured against near neighbours Slovenia. That result began their ascent of the rankings but not before they'd suffered three months listed as the worst in the world.

For some countries, the task of striving to win a game, or at least avoid defeat, in order to climb above the foot of the world rankings was seemingly too much of a hardship. Over the years, several teams who have found themselves stuck at the bottom have managed to escape by the simple ruse of not playing at all for extended periods. Their inactivity saw them disappear from the rankings altogether, a shaming fact in itself perhaps, but a rather less public one. Hidden from view, these countries avoided the label of worst in the world by not exposing themselves to the possibility of defeat. A cunning plan if ever there was one.

Various countries in the far-flung corners of world football have achieved this notable, if ignoble feat. In Asia, Afghanistan and Papua New Guinea both escaped the bottom ranking in this manner, although in Papua New Guinea's case they first had to endure three long years propping up the rankings before being finally, mercifully cut loose. Having ultimately rid themselves of the unwanted label in this rather pacifistic manner, barely two months later they returned to action with a bang and roundly thrashed the Cook Islands 4-0. A return to the ranking saw them well clear of last place.

African side Sao Tome e Principe took things a little further having dropped out of the rankings at the end of 2007 after a year as the worst team in the world. Their sabbatical from the FIFA list was rather more prolonged than Papua New Guinea's had been with a further four years passing by without any international action. Had they remained on the rankings during that period, they would have rivalled Montserrat and San Marino for the lengthiest spells as basement dwellers. As it was, they sat comfortably away from view leaving others to carry that tag. When they returned to action in an Africa Cup of Nations qualifying tie in 2011 they avoided defeat in securing a 1-1 draw with Congo. The subsequent ranking publication saw Sao Tome reappear in 192nd place, fully twelve positions above those languishing at the bottom.

Missing for even longer than Sao Tome was the Caribbean nation of the Bahamas. They endured a three-month stint at the foot of the rankings in 1993 after which they vanished from the listing. An absence of nigh on six years kept them unencumbered by being highlighted as the worst before they returned to action in 1999. When they did so, they chose their opponents wisely, taking on and beating the populace-challenged Turks and Caicos Islands 3-0 and re-joining the rankings well clear of the bottom.

Their vanquished opponents that day also found themselves stranded near the foot of the table following their World Cup humbling by Haiti in early 2004. Defeats in those clashes left the islanders reeling and kept them out of action for a couple of years, preferring to focus on youth development and improving infrastructure rather than being resoundingly hammered internationally. During that time, their remaining ranking points gradually dwindled away until they could no longer avoid the final sliding slump to the bottom of the pile.

When they did resurface once more, two and a half years later, they ran straight into a thumping defeat by Cuba in a Caribbean Cup qualifying group in Havana. Just two days later, they had more success in finally picking on someone closer to their own size, taking on the Cayman Islands. A comfortable 2-0 saw their spell as worst in the world end in fine style, at least for the time being.

There is clearly more than one method of skinning the cat that is the 'worst in the world' tag. Simply winning or drawing a football match may seem the obvious means of escape, though some of the examples above prove there are other ways too. Yet the one truth will always remain. To be listed above last place you need to achieve some semblance of success on the field of play.

Chapter 6: Bringing in the Experts

In the decade since their unforgettable rout at the hands of Australia, American Samoa's fortunes had not improved one jot. In seventeen subsequent matches over the intervening years they had lost every single one, conceding one hundred and twenty-five times and scoring just four in return. The vagaries of the evolving ranking methods used by FIFA meant that American Samoa hadn't been ranked in last place for the whole decade that had passed since the beating in 2001, but they had sunk to last place in 2005 and had remained there ever since.

Two further World Cup qualifying campaigns had come and gone in a flurry of more heavy defeats – fifteen conceded to Vanuatu, twelve to the Solomon Islands, eleven to Fiji – as the team blindly continued repeating their haphazard and unschooled methods. But, with another World Cup campaign imminent, they would be better prepared than ever before. The previous coaching efforts of well-intentioned local amateurs had seen them repeatedly flounder. Now they sought to bring in some old-world expertise to assist the local enthusiasm, albeit only briefly. Would the outcome be any different?

There is a clear rationale as to why teams so unused to even a hint of success, and hampered by their own limited ability and expertise, would look beyond their shores for a bit of footballing know-how. Indeed, this is a phenomenon hardly limited to the weakest of FIFA's members, but something that many a country sees as its best method of reaching beyond its current level. What would be unthinkable to the real elite, the likes of Germany, Argentina, Spain and Brazil - naming a foreign coach - is quite commonplace amongst many other nations.

It doesn't always work, of course. For every Guus Hiddink with South Korea in 2002, or Jurgen Klinsmann with the USA in recent years, there is a Fabio Capello with England and Russia, or a Berti Vogts with Scotland, or Sven-Goran Eriksson with any number of teams. Further down the ladder though, the effects can be more marked. This is due, in part, to a far greater step up in the knowledge levels and more crucially exposure to, and experience of, a higher level of competition than most local coaches could ever have managed.

American Samoa's enthusiastic but limited locals had been complemented over the years with some help from overseas. Returning from Seattle where he lived and coached, Larry Mana'o was part of the Samoan diaspora in the United States but was only too willing to return home to help the team. His local knowledge and cultural understanding would, he felt, help him in his task, in contrast to some of the previous coaches who had taken the reins for short, sharp stints.

In amongst the local coaches there had been a couple of Englishmen who had taken charge for various unsuccessful stages of American Samoa's recent past, bringing with them a level of technical expertise and credentials far in excess of anything the locals could offer. But they hadn't been able to coax anything other than more heavy defeats out of the team. According to Mana'o it was a question of understanding. 'A lot of people have tried to come here and help them. They do it technically correct, but the problem is they don't understand the Samoan culture,' he commented. 'They have such big hearts, they'll play through pain, they'll walk through walls. They're very religious, they have incredible faith. They'll do anything for their country and for their families.'[66]

American Samoa's problems weren't limited to the concerns of tactics and morale however. With an unemployment rate approaching twenty-five per cent, a great number of the island's youth would leave for the United States, frequently to join the US military or to simply find work. Mana'o had done the same, and like him, for any footballers among the expats, returning to the South Pacific for a likely thrashing wasn't an easy or necessarily desirable thing to do.

Economic troubles were compounded by natural factors too. American Samoa was hit by a devastating tsunami in September 2009, which left thirty-one people dead. Among the damaged homes and offices, the national football team's training centre was also destroyed. With nowhere to train and very little money to rebuild, American Samoa, like Montserrat and East Timor before them, turned to the FIFA GOAL program for funding. They even got a visit from Sepp Blatter himself to inaugurate the new facilities, who regaled the watching dignitaries with some warm-worded idealism: 'Football as a vehicle for hope is not a vain concept, and the inauguration of this centre, which was destroyed by the tsunami, is proof of this. Now more than ever, football needs to be used as a school of life, an educational tool to build a better future for the young people of American Samoa.'[67] Fine aims of course, but football inspiration trickles down from the top. Seeing their national team thumped from pillar to post by a succession of less than stellar opponents is hardly conducive to inspiring participation.

Two years on from that tsunami, and just three months before the World Cup campaign was due to commence, American Samoa's players gathered to take part in their first international action in four years. Since bowing out of the 2010 World Cup qualifiers in mid-2007, naturally at the first hurdle, American Samoa had been in hibernation, stranded as one of a cluster of teams at the bottom of the world rankings. What had previously doubled as the opening round of Oceania World Cup qualification, the South Pacific Games football competition pitched a host of idyllic-sounding nations together for South Seas supremacy and was held in Noumea, New Caledonia, in August 2011. American Samoa may have been the lowliest on the FIFA rankings, but at this tournament there were also teams representing island territories yet to earn the distinction of FIFA membership, namely Kiribati and Tuvalu. In short, they were beatable opposition.

It was the team from the collection of reef islands and atolls that make up Tuvalu who would provide American Samoa's opposition in their opening match. In football terms, notable only for the fact that they were the first non-FIFA nation to play a World Cup qualifier when a previous South Pacific tournament was combined with qualification for the global tournament, they surely represented a great opportunity for the winless wonders of American Samoa to record a first ever victory. Alas if they were to capture that elusive win, it would be one that would have no bearing on their ranking within FIFA given their unaffiliated opposition.

Larry Mana'o had travelled back to the South Pacific from Seattle to coach the team, hoping to build some positive momentum before the impending World Cup qualifiers. Also returning from Seattle for this tournament was Nicky Salapu, once more taking his place in the firing line. He had been the youthful goalkeeper conceding the record-breaking goals haul in *that* match in 2001. After the trauma of that catastrophic and devastating World Cup baptism of fire, Salapu had returned to his Seattle home and thrown himself into the local football scene, playing several nights a week as well as coaching two school teams. Many years had passed now, but the psychological torment and the destructive impact it had wielded on his life remained.

'I've been carrying it now for nearly eleven years,' said Salapu. 'It was emotionally... dramatic. Terrible. It was the terrible thing that happened to me. This was the worst thing ever. But things happen for a reason. Maybe that's why, to challenge us.'[68]

Confidence was high. It was their first tournament in four years, but the feeling was that this set of players had the capability to do what no other team representing American Samoa had ever done before: win a match. As summed up by the twenty-two year-old school teacher and national team captain, defender Laitama Amisome, ahead of departure for the tournament in New Caledonia: 'I believe that this is the best team taking the name of American Samoa to represent the island. We're going to show them that we're better than before. I know we can win. Trust me.' Also confident was the volunteer coach Larry Mana'o. 'We want to make history this week.'[69]

Following the dramas at that tournament were a UK film crew capturing the hopes and dreams of the American Samoans for a documentary film, *Next Goal Wins*, as they ventured into action once more. 'It seemed obvious that the players in a team that had never won anything, but continued to play in the face of defeat time and time again, must love the sport more than anyone,' explained one of the film's directors Steve Jamison.[70]

As the opening match against Tuvalu progressed, Larry Mana'o, pacing up and down the sidelines, gradually became more and more frantic. Chances had come and gone for his team, but unused to the fleeting glimpses of goal, the players fluffed their lines every time. At the other end, Nicky Salapu once more leapt from one side of his goal to the other, attempting to stem the tide that flowed freely through his undisciplined defence. His efforts were as futile as King Canute's in that regard. When Tuvalu eventually took the lead, Mana'o, watching on helplessly, summed his feelings up with a neat

'Ah, shit.' In the end, four goals found their way into the American Samoan net as Tuvalu recorded the biggest win in their history.

Another four-goal defeat to the Solomon Islands saw Mana'o, his earlier optimism now long gone, angrily shouting post-match, 'That was not the plan!' By the time both Vanuatu and New Caledonia hit them for eight, Mana'o managed to put a remarkably positive spin on things as his team sat crestfallen in the dressing room afterwards. 'They needed nine goals today. We gave them only eight. It's a step, a step in the right direction.' I'm not sure even he believed it.[71]

The team returned home to lick their wounds, just as they had done every other time they'd played, thoroughly defeated in spite of their prior, and as it turned out misplaced, optimism. For all their enthusiasm, American Samoa's fortunes had continued in a frustratingly familiar vein to all that had gone before, leaving the players demoralised yet again. Although Nicky Salapu made numerous saves, he still conceded twenty-six goals in their five matches, with not even one to celebrate at the other end. For Salapu, enough was enough. 'I really wanted to change the history, and I wanted to win,' he noted as the tournament concluded. 'And I can't change the fact that it's going to be the last moment of soccer for me for the national team. But you know, you never know...' His voice trailed away as his frustration gave way to the disappointment and regret of unfulfilled dreams.[72] For a goalkeeper so used to picking the ball out of his own net and so synonymous with heavy defeat, he made an astonishing number of saves in his time, all the way back to that Australia match in 2001. But after a decade of playing for the national team, Nicky retired to Seattle, his dreams unrealised, having never won a game with American Samoa.

Mana'o headed back to Seattle too, still wishing that one day his national team could 'just get that one goal that would be like a win to them.' With the World Cup qualifiers looming large on the horizon, the American Samoans finally acknowledged that simply repeating the failed efforts of the past would, in mirroring Einstein's definition of insanity, merely produce the same results as before. This time they would get in some expertise from a far higher level than ever before.

* * * * *

'When I got here, I had never seen a lower standard of international football,' said Thomas Rongen in his gruff, gravelly, Dutch-accented delivery.[73] It was officially the lowest standard in all of international football as American Samoa, still deliriously punch-drunk from their record-breaking Australian-inflicted trauma (more than a decade earlier) were firmly embedded in last place in the FIFA rankings. 'I inherited this team and there were five guys literally thirty or forty pounds overweight,' Rongen added. 'There was no way they could even play ten minutes if they wanted to compete at this kind of level.'[74]

Ten years on it may have been but the damage inflicted by that World Cup qualifying nightmare was still very real as American Samoa prepared to enter the World Cup fray once more. And yet there was an air of, if not optimism as such, then professionalism at least. In the lush verdant surroundings and gently swaying palm trees that envelop the stadium in Apia, the capital city of neighbouring Samoa, the players of American Samoa lined up to hear their national anthem ahead of the their opening fixture and readied themselves to step once more unto the breach of World Cup qualifying.

Looking on from the sidelines, American Samoa's Dutch coach Thomas Rongen was observing proceedings, and stood anxiously waiting for the start of his first match in charge. For Rongen, just as for many of his players, this World Cup adventure represented a step into the unknown, a leap of faith, and a severe shock to the system.

'I had to learn some serious lessons in the beginning,' he said. 'I thought I would go in there hard, training twice a day and the rest, but that plainly didn't work with this squad. So I immersed myself in their culture, threw out the books and developed a new training plan.'[75]

Thomas Rongen, a fifty-five year-old Dutchman, arrived in American Samoa with just three weeks to go before the World Cup qualifiers. Slight and wiry, with a flash of white-grey hair, what he lacked in physical stature he more than made up for with his manner and demeanour. He was the archetypal football man, straight-talking, charismatic and direct. He'd played with and coached some of the best. He came with pedigree and experience. And he was now coach of the worst team in the world.

'I don't see it as an obscure job. It is a unique opportunity to do something that's a once in a lifetime gig,' he explained. That opportunity came about when the president of the United States Soccer Federation, Sunil Gulati, met with officials from the Oceania Football Confederation and the federation of American Samoa to discuss ways in which the USSF could assist some of the South Pacific's developing nations. The American federation has typically offered a range of support over the years, from clinics for coaches and players to technical expertise, but American Samoa's need was for something more than that.

'We talked about some things that we might be able to do with American Samoa,' recalled Gulati in an interview with *ESPN*. 'And of particular interest to them was some coaching assistance. That eventually led to a process not just where we would send someone over to work on some clinics, but where one of our coaches would actually coach the team in World Cup qualifying.'[76]

The USSF placed a job advert amongst the host of coaches it employed at various levels for the temporary role. There was only one applicant, a coach at the US national Under 20s team, Thomas Rongen. Having come through as a young defensive midfielder in the youth system at his hometown Ajax Amsterdam, he unfortunately failed to make the grade in the first team. Instead, he moved to America and the razzmatazz of the North American Soccer League in 1979 where he was something of a journeyman player, moving between various teams and playing alongside and against some of the world's true greats. He played with his hero Johan Cruyff in both Los Angeles and Washington, and took on the likes of Franz Beckenbauer and George Best.

Staying in the US after his playing days were over, he went into coaching and was a part of the coaching staff for the USA at the 1998 World Cup before becoming Head Coach at several MLS sides. He was later hired by the USSF to coach the Under 20s national team. In American Samoa, he saw the opportunity to coach a senior national team, albeit the lowliest national team of them all. 'My wife's first reaction was, "Are you daft?"', Rongen confessed. 'In saying that, everybody looks for opportunities and challenges. I love to travel and take on new opportunities and this was a unique one to say the least. They were ranked last so I felt they couldn't get any worse.'[77]

He was in for quite a shock on arrival. 'The soccer IQ level is very low, lower than I've ever encountered,'[78] he said. Rongen had initially attempted to stick to his plans for training twice a day and as a confirmed atheist, saw no reason to adjust his schedule to allow his players to attend daily church services. In a deeply religious country, this set him on an early collision course before he realised that an understanding of the local culture and customs would be a more successful approach. He quickly grasped the need to blend his expertise with the local styles and culture. If an outsider is to be successful, the local aspect is always key. It's never a simple case of bringing in an experienced coach, instilling a football ideal from the big leagues and getting instant success. The character of a country and its people must always be accounted for, and Rongen understood this.

Failing to grasp that concept is a mistake that many a country and coach had made when seeking a quick fix or instant boost. Shipping in the likes of Sven-Goran Eriksson on the eve of a World Cup, as the Ivory Coast did in 2010, to oversee a team that had been steadily built over many years was doomed to fail without a proper degree of integration and understanding. A great generation of players just needed some crucial direction, went the thinking, with a chance of progressing to the knock-out rounds theirs for the taking. But football, and indeed human nature, isn't as simple as that. Put simply, both parties need to 'get' each other. With that in mind, a chain-smoking Dutchman from the USSF may not seem a likely match for the sleepy Pacific island of American Samoa, but gradually in the few weeks before the World Cup qualifiers, they grew together.

Soon, the lifelong atheist was joining in his team's daily prayers and songs and finding a soothing sense of spirituality, if not religion. But more than that, he was rewarded with a reminder of the pure joy of football. A memory of the game he knew and fell in love with as a child in the Netherlands, with players who competed not for glory, but simply for the joy of playing – a far cry from the cynical, professional world of football to which he had become accustomed. 'It is pure, it can't get any purer,' he said warmly. 'These guys actually play because they love the game. They get zero, nothing. It's pretty amazing.'[79]

In those short, few weeks before the World Cup matches kicked off, Rongen set about trying to get his players into some sort of shape and worked on passing on as much technical and tactical insight as possible. Rather shocked at the standard of player he had to work with, he sought to supplement the local squad by bringing in some American Samoan players living in the US who had competed at a higher level. 'I knew no amount of training was going to get the team to a competitive level that quickly, so I found four American Samoan players who lived in the US, and, when I reminded our existing team that our aim was to win, they quickly bought into the idea.'[80]

Rawlston Masaniai was one such player. Born and raised in Phoenix, Arizona, Masaniai qualified for American Samoa through his grandfather, although he himself hadn't been to the islands in twenty years, since he was a small child. He'd played football to a high level in college in the US, and briefly flirted with a club in Germany though his trial there didn't lead to a contract offer. He jumped at the chance to fulfil his dream of playing in the World Cup, no matter what the level.

Two members of the US armed forces, the brothers Ramin and Diamond Ott, were also persuaded to return to American Samoa for the qualifiers. The Ott brothers are the perfect example of how a significant proportion of the island's young chose to escape the mass unemployment and limited opportunities afforded them at home by signing up with the US military. Ramin Ott used up all three weeks of his annual leave at the same time to be there, and had to leave behind his heavily pregnant wife and young child to realise his World Cup dream. His travels with the US Army had afforded him the opportunity to play more football at a higher level, notably whilst posted to South Korea, as to make him a valuable addition.

'The off island players will add another dimension, a more mature dimension, which I think is good,' commented Rongen in *Next Goal Wins*. 'They want to help this team out to get to a level where they could actually maybe score a goal or win a game, which hasn't happened in the history of this island.'[81]

Also returning from the States for one final hurrah was Nicky Salapu, the goalkeeper who had suffered more than anyone from the demons of a decade before. He was persuaded to abandon his international retirement by Rongen, and to return to the fold to give the World Cup qualifiers one last go. 'I called him and asked him to come back, to shed his demons,' said Rongen. 'It was a big gamble. I had no idea when I called him how driven he would be, how motivated he was. I had one goalie who could have probably done an adequate job for us, but Nicky was the only player from the 31-0 loss. Everyone knew of him. He became a true inspiration – almost like we owe it to Nicky to work hard and do something special.'[82]

'I needed somebody there who could represent the battle scars of the team,' Rongen continued. 'When training didn't go well, I just had to remind them that Nicky was here and that he had been reliving that game for all these years, and if he can exorcise his demons then so can the team.'[83]

And what demons they were. 'He asked me if I wanted to remove the embarrassment of that game, the 31-0 to Australia,' Salapu recalled. 'He said this was a good moment, that he was a professional coach, that we had good players and some from here in the States. He kept telling me all these things. I was working hard for my family, they really needed me. I didn't feel like going. When he told me all these things, and telling me he wanted to put the embarrassment of the 31-0 to the side and become winners. I was like, "ok, this will be the best moment to go back and come out of the embarrassment." I'm glad he called me.'[84]

'Those guys have been in some battles, and none more so than Nicky,' Rongen added. 'For him, it's all about showing the world that this country, not only himself but the team, can do something. That we can win a game. That we aren't losers.'[85]

So Nicky Salapu took leave from his job repairing cables for AT&T and put his gloves on once more. Reversing his retirement decision and leaving his family was clearly a tough choice to make, but if he was ever to finally vanquish the ghosts of his past, he had to face them one last time. 'I want to win a game. If we win, I'd die a happy person,' he added.[86] 'I'm just trying to prove we're not the same team anymore. Going back, it's a big sacrifice. This tournament is very important for me. This is something that I was dreaming about, you know. I love my family very much and this is the chance for me to make them proud.'[87] Behind his words, there was always the underlying sense that his fragile state of mind would struggle to cope with another humiliation.

The mental trauma waged by the memory of all those defeats lingered not only in Salapu's psyche, but also in the minds of many of his younger colleagues who may not have been a part of the 31-0 defeat, but had known nothing other than defeat with the national team. 'A lot of the guys who have lost every game – not 2-1, or 3-2 but they'd get their asses kicked on a regular basis. So there was a defeatist attitude which I really had to change,' commented Rongen. He had to fight the all enveloping attitude going into games that if they could keep the score below ten, then they had done well. But it was Salapu who was the most conflicted. 'This guy,' Rongen said with a shake of the head, 'has got some major demons going on, totally driven by the thirty-one-nothing, erasing this for himself and his family. He is so preoccupied about it, almost crazed. There's some incredible scars.'[88]

* * * * *

'The guys would get up at 4.30 a.m. from sleeping on the floor, no mattress, in one big room, and I would take eight guys and go down to the docks to the tuna boats,' said Rongen. 'They would work their tails off for eight hours, come back in the afternoon and get their butts kicked again by me, and always with a smile on their face.'[89]

This was the routine for the three weeks of intensive training ahead of the World Cup matches. They trained every day after a long day at work, or in many cases at school. But it was a more focused, and intense, level of training to any they'd done before. Rongen actually shortened the sessions to allow them to be more intense, while leaving plenty of time to work on the players' mental attitudes. 'I worked on the mental side as much as I did on the technical, tactical and fitness side,' he said. 'And was able to put a team on the field that became competitive, that believed they could win a game. I think they had reached a point where I could look them in the eyes before the game and they actually thought they could compete with those teams. That was a big thing.'[90]

Rongen demanded total commitment and dedication from his players, on and off the pitch, something that acted as a bit of a wake-up call to one or two. Anyone not meeting these standards would swiftly find themselves out of the team. As Salapu recalled, 'This made a lot of people think, "Oh, this guy is serious."' This attitude cultivated a newfound level of professionalism, the likes of which had been alien to the American Samoans beforehand.

The weeks ticked by with alarming rapidity, and ready or not, the World Cup qualifiers were soon upon them. Prior to departing the American Samoan capital Pago Pago for the short hop to Samoa, Rongen gave an emotional, moving team talk to his players sat around the al-fresco dining table at the team's training base. Revealing to his squad how he had lost his daughter eight years earlier in a car accident at the tender age of eighteen, he drew on that memory when, through a cracking, wavering, grief-stricken voice, he implored his players, to: 'Cherish what you have right now. Make it happen by going out there and playing as hard as you can. Show me the American Samoan warrior, and I'll show you how to win.'[91]

* * * * *

The national stadium on the outskirts of Apia, Samoa, is not one of world football's most iconic stadiums. In fact, as described by James Montague in *Thirty-One Nil*, "It would be wrong to call the J. S. Blatter Stadium a stadium as such."[92] Yet it is frequently in such settings – sparse and simple, surrounded by rolling hills, snow-peaked mountains or in Apia's case, a smattering of palm trees, densely forested hills and barely any spectator facilities – that the exploits of the worst in the world are played out. Unlike their footballing superiors playing in modern, often identikit, soulless stadiums, those at the other end of the spectrum frequently compete in the most idyllic of settings, as though the beauty of the surroundings are trying to compensate for the absence of it on the pitch.

The one small stand, with its handful of covered seats, provided the only shelter from the blazing sun or the expected occasional downpour, as this four-way tournament coincided with the start of the rainy season. The team benches were little more than two blue tents covered in FIFA livery either side of the half-way line, housing a few fold-away chairs. At each end, the pitch was backed by a small grassy slope, with one or two palm trees dotted at one end, and a thick wall of deep green trees at the other to lend a suitably exotic air to proceedings.

Here four of the weakest national teams in the world would battle each other to live out, even briefly, their dreams of reaching the global show in Brazil. For American Samoa, the dream was a more realistic one: simply not losing. The four lowliest ranked of Oceania's World Cup entrants would play this first round group with the winner progressing on to the next stage to face the relative big boys of New Zealand, Tahiti and the Solomon Islands. Joining American Samoa were their hosts and neighbours Samoa, also ranked joint last on FIFA's rankings at the time. Tonga sat one place above those two in the rankings, while the tournament favourites, the Cook Islands, sat a giddy eight places higher at 196th. American Samoa had never so much as scored a goal against any of them.

'We win the little battles, we win the war,' Rongen's firm, deep voice asserted to his team as they steeled themselves to walk out to face Tonga in their opening match. 'And it will be a war for ninety minutes. We respect them, but we don't fear them. And we kick their ass. It's peace afterwards.'[93] He had earlier confessed to having his doubts about how his team would react: 'When that whistle blows will they choke again? Will they literally give goals away?'[94]

His team marched out dressed in crisp white and red shirts in front of just a handful of spectators to the strains of the warbling FIFA anthem alongside the Tongan opposition. Their opponents had also looked abroad for coaching expertise. Chris Williams, a twenty-five year-old Australian, was the youngest coach to ever take charge of a full FIFA national team and was significantly younger than several of his team. As the American Samoan anthem played, the players turned to face their flag, every one of them with hands on heart. Emotions were running deep, not least for Nicky Salapu. He could be forgiven if his thoughts wandered back to that harrowing evening in Coffs Harbour a decade before. Nobody had suffered quite like he had. And there he was again, about to step into the World Cup qualifying firing line once more. Standing taller than them all, singing the anthem with pride, was the team's elegant and leggy centre-back, Johnny Saelua. With his long hair tied back into a pony-tail and wearing eye-liner and make-up, Saelua was no ordinary player. He wasn't known to his team-mates as Johnny. To them she was Jaiyah, and was about to become the World Cup's first ever transgender player.

Having impressed during training to such an extent, Jaiyah Saelua was the surprise selection for the opening match. It was some upturn in fortunes for the twenty-three year-old performing arts student. Only a couple of weeks earlier, Rongen had praised her contribution to the squad and its morale but felt she was unlikely to get any minutes on the pitch once the action kicked off. And yet there she was, having earned her place and about to make history. 'Can you imagine that in England or Spain?' Rongen stated before the match. 'I've really got a female starting at centre back.'[95]

Technically, Jaiyah belongs to Samoa's third gender, the *fa'afafine*, which translates as "way of the woman" and is completely accepted in Samoan culture. 'We have two spirits: the man's spirit and the woman's spirit,' Jaiyah explained. 'We can do what the men do and what the women do. I'm just a soccer player, even though I run like a girl on the field. But I'm not a male or a female, I'm a soccer player.'[96] As she suggested, on the field she is all flailing arms, flowing locks and seemingly uncoordinated legs. But when a ball is there to be won, she is tough and uncompromising. To her teammates, she was just another one of the team. 'They don't make me feel any different because I am the way I am,' she said. 'I can't let them down. I hope I can inspire people, not only transgender but anybody who feels different in their society or community. If there's something you love to do, go out and don't let anybody stop you from chasing after your dreams.'[97]

She was no stranger to setting records, having first played for the national team aged just fourteen. Oddly, she was now lining up alongside her original football coach from school; none other than Nicky Salapu. Whilst fully accepted in American Samoa, she had faced discrimination when playing at college in Hawaii, and hadn't been selected to play for the national team by any of the previous foreign managers. But Rongen – 'the first coach to call me Jaiyah on the field, and not Johnny' – had been won over by her dedication, desire and skills during the lead up to these games.

The match began in frantic style as the weeks of anticipation were finally replaced by reality. The action got under way and the adrenalin surged. On the sidelines, Rongen, wearing a cap belonging to his daughter, paced up and down barking out a constant stream of clipped instructions: 'Organised', 'Stay Focused', 'Defence!' As the frenetic early exchanges subsided and the game's patterns settled, something strange began to happen. Something that had rarely, if ever, happened before. American Samoa were having repeated attacks and efforts on goal and were dominating proceedings. At the back, Jaiyah Saelua was keeping the defensive line tight, and any efforts that did break through were comfortably dealt with by Nicky Salapu behind her, who was playing with an assuredness and confidence and thwarting all efforts at a Tongan breakthrough.

In one of American Samoa's early attacks, a shot from just outside the Tongan box, by Ramin Ott, hit the adjoining corner of post and crossbar. The thud of the ball, having come so close to giving American Samoa the lead, caused a gasp from the smattering of spectators and several sharp intakes of breath from those on the American Samoan bench. They were getting closer and closer. So near, and yet, and yet... Straightaway, the ball broke for the Tongans who raced upfield on the counter attack and found their striker all alone inside the box with only Salapu to beat, but the keeper stood tall and made the save. More sharp intakes of breath on the bench.

Shortly before half time with the match still goalless, some nice passing possession in midfield led to a ball forward from Jaiyah to Ramin Ott, who fired a rather speculative effort from a good thirty-five yards out. It was a weak effort that bounced in the penalty area before it reached the goal. But the bounce confused the diving Tongan keeper, springing up from the grass higher than he expected. In true comic style, the ball passed through his hands, and hit him in the face. As he crashed to the ground, he could only turn in despair to see the ball nestling in the net behind him. American Samoa had scored a goal.

After all the years of heartbreak, of endless beatings and scarcely a goal to celebrate, scoring in such a manner seemed oddly appropriate. The players ran around screaming in sheer disbelief as though unsure of what to do. They'd prepared thoroughly for this match but didn't seem to have any plan for what had just happened. Many of the players bore down on Rongen and soon the whole squad ended up piled up in a delirious heap in celebration in front of their coach.

As the second half wore on, the nerves increased as it became apparent that victory was a real possibility. With just over quarter of an hour to go, that possibility edged a step closer. A loose Tongan header in midfield was seized upon by Justin Mana'o in the midfield. He sent a high, looping ball through to the seventeen-year-old Shalom Luani who raced clear of the static defence. Luani and the Tongan keeper both bore down on the ball and appeared set on a crunching collision. Luani's will was the stronger and he was there slightly quicker, getting a foot to the ball moments before the Tongan keeper sent him sprawling and squealing in pain. He collapsed to the ground, clearly hurt, but he had succeeded in clipping the ball over the keeper. He glanced up to see it nestling in the net for a second goal. Victory was now so close they could almost touch it. Luani was hobbling, but carried on.

On the sidelines, Rongen tried to keep the mounting excitement in check. 'This game is not over guys,' he implored, attempting to keep his players fully focused on the task at hand. As the final moments ticked by agonisingly slowly, the American Samoan players visibly tired. Their play – sharp, intense and snappy before – became increasingly loose, while players started going down with cramp left, right and centre. Tonga pulled a goal back with a fine back post header with minutes remaining to heighten the nerves yet further. As the clock reached ninety minutes, with the play from both teams increasingly desperate, ragged and chaotic, Tonga's striker was put clean through with Jaiyah Saelua in hot pursuit desperately trying to cover. Nicky Salapu charged from his goal to challenge the onrushing striker. Win or draw, it was all in this moment.

Salapu got there first but the ball broke to another Tongan forward, with Salapu now stranded. The ball was nudged goalwards, but there to clear it and maintain the slender lead was Jaiyah Saelua who prodded the ball away. Seconds later, it was whacked clear into touch to the audible delight of those biting their nails on the bench. The players celebrated with gusto, as though it was another goal. Nicky Salapu later described the moment: 'All of a sudden, I was "Where is the ball? Oh my God, I got beat." When I looked back, the ball was already coming back [clear], and I saw Jaiyah standing there.'[98]

At the final whistle just moments later, the American Samoan players, without the strength of their earlier goal scoring celebrations, stood arms aloft in celebration, or sunk to their knees in sheer relief, all remaining energy now exhausted. After thirty defeats, American Samoa had finally won a game. Nicky Salapu buried his face deep into his gloved hands at the final whistle, stifling his screams. After all his hurt and humiliation, he found it hard to take things in: 'It's like a miracle, but it's not a miracle. It's very emotional right now, it's overwhelming.'

His teammates performed a celebratory post match *haka*, the *siva tau*, in the centre of the pitch. It was led by the captain, a shirtless and almost delirious Laitama Amisome, and was delivered with a gut-wrenching level of intensity. The joy, the relief, the release was palpable. Salapu stood to one side and watched, lost in his own thoughts. 'Finally, I'm going to put the past behind me,' he said. 'I can live my life again. I feel like I'm just released from prison.'[99]

Rongen was equally effusive in his thoughts on Salapu's redemption. 'The first thing after the game, he looked to me,' he said of Salapu. 'He was crying, and said, "I can now tell my children that I'm a winner", and that is bigger than the game itself quite frankly.'[100]

'We've never won a game [before]. We win, we score. To me that's history,' he continued. 'This is going to be part of soccer history, just like the thirty-one-nothing against Australia is part of history. We've got two games to play, maybe we've got a chance to do something special beyond this one game, but let's enjoy this one right now. It's the most rewarding, the most satisfying win that I've ever had.'[101] Having made world headlines a decade before, after their ultimate humiliation, they once more made the news from the *New York Times* to the *BBC World Service*, this time significantly more upbeat.

Next, they would face the highest ranked team in the group, the Cook Islands; a team containing several New Zealanders of island heritage who played semi-professionally in the New Zealand leagues. And yet, under their New Zealand coach Shane Rufer, brother of the Oceania player of the century, Wynton Rufer, they had fallen to defeat in their opening match against the hosts Samoa. Amid rumours of mutiny in the camp, Rufer was sacked by his federation's president, pitchside, just minutes before the American Samoa match.

Without him, his former Cook Islands team failed to improve on their opening performance. They struggled to contain the repeated waves of American Samoan attack, as the new belief which now coursed through the veins of each player carried them forwards once more. It was as though all the years that had gone before, all of the defeats, all the anguish, had been washed away, cleansed by that seismic first victory. A dominant first half was capped off when Shalom Luani, his leg thankfully unscathed following his opening match heroics, broke through the middle and slid the ball home. American Samoa were in the lead again, and once more it was fully deserved.

This time, though, there was to be no fairy tale ending, and sadly it was the old trait of self-destruction that was to blame. A terrific second half header by American Samoan defender Tala Luvu, from a lofted free-kick, arrowed past the stranded keeper and nestled in the net. Unfortunately for Luvu, it was past his own keeper, Nicky Salapu. Under no pressure at all, the Cook Islands had been gifted an equaliser. Repeated raids forward for the rest of the game saw American Samoa unable to regain the lead that their play had deserved. The match ended in a 1-1 draw that could, and should, have been so much more. It was still another first, their first ever draw, and the overall mood in the camp remained upbeat; at least it was once Rongen's initial anger at letting victory slip had subsided.

This set up a grand finale, a South Pacific classic. With Tonga and the Cook Islands now both unable to win the group, and Samoa having drawn with Tonga, it would all come down to Samoa versus American Samoa: a Samoan *clasico*.

Both teams were ranked joint last in FIFA's rankings at the time of the match, but that equality didn't tell the full story. Samoa hadn't played a match since the last World Cup qualifiers four years earlier and had sunk in the rankings as their previous points tally was gradually expunged. Ranked level they may have been, but Samoa were the team with pedigree with several professional players plying their trade in the leagues of Australia and New Zealand. After all that had gone before, American Samoa would need to muster one more miracle if they were to come out on top. Having wiped away the demons of their past humiliations, they faced a wholly unexpected and entirely different challenge. They were trying to become champions.

Thomas Rongen's opposite number had his own connection to American Samoa's darkest football moment. Tunoa Lui had been the American Samoa coach back in 2001, and like Salapu, had been carrying the weight of that debacle ever since. It was 'one of the worst nights of my life,' and had caused him untold grief. Public humiliation was one thing, being almost unemployable as a result was another altogether. As the coach that had presided over the biggest defeat in international football he was scarcely in demand, but he gradually rebuilt his career in his native Samoa and was back in World Cup action once more, seeking his own emancipation.

Given the relative goal differences, American Samoa needed a win to top the group and progress through to the next round. Samoa just needed a draw. The match was preceded by a heavy tropical downpour, which for a time threatened to cause a postponement. So much rain had fallen that ever since Tonga had beaten the Cook Islands earlier in the day, a team of men had been vainly trying to drain the pitch using a haphazard combination of brushes, buckets and sticks. But, by kick-off, the heavens had eased sufficiently at least for the game to go ahead.

A rather larger crowd than had been seen in the earlier matches meant that the small stand at least was full. The rest of the perimeter was dotted with the occasional ball boy, unable to shelter from the rain, hoping that the ball would come their way once in a while. The pitch was muddy and heavy which made for hard going. Salapu, still making saves, making blocks, tipping the ball over the bar, and claiming crosses, was a man inspired once more as he began to accumulate layers of mud on his previously clean kit. He needed to be in fine form though. The match was all flowing one way, and that was steadily and inexorably towards his goal as Samoa's greater quality shone through, even in such difficult playing conditions. His efforts kept his team in contention as Samoa tried to finish the contest off early.

After a tense, goalless first half, Rongen's plan to keep things tight before going for the win late on was still alive. They'd clung on despite all the pressure they been subjected to and now Rongen looked to reassure his team. He told them, 'We are exactly where we

93

wanted to be, so relax.' His plan was to bring on the pacey forward Diamond Ott for the latter stages of the match as the opposition tired, and to go for it with everything they had. With twenty minutes left, the time had come for this pre-planned move, and American Samoa pushed forwards in search of a winner.

In the very dying embers of the match, still goalless, a neat through-ball put the speedy Diamond Ott clear of the Samoan defence. He was the quickest man on the pitch, and the scrambling, panicked defenders were unable to get near him. Rongen's plan looked to be working to perfection. The Samoan keeper raced out to face Ott, but the forward shot the ball past him, as Rongen yelled 'Go Diamond! Go Diamond! Go!' from the bench. The ball rolled across the muddy turf looking for all the world to be heading for the back of the net as Diamond Ott began to wheel away in anticipated celebration. But, instead, the ball rebounded off the post to the safety of the quickly backtracking Samoan defence. Mere inches, the thickness of the post, had separated American Samoa from victory and a place in the next round. Several American Samoan players fell to their knees, clearly thinking their best chance had come and gone.

They were right. Samoa attacked immediately following this let off and broke towards the other end. The American Samoan players weren't covering as they had been before, as though they'd all begun to celebrate the goal that so nearly was. As his players desperately tried to recover their positions and halt the Samoan break, on the sidelines, Rongen's slightly panicked voice yelled, 'The game is not over. The game is not over.' Seconds later it may as well have been. Samoa's striker fired through Salapu's legs with one of the last kicks of the match, denying him a first ever international clean-sheet. The win would be Samoa's.

In such circumstances, the defeat was hard to take. There were tears, there were bowed heads, but there was immense pride in how far they had come in so short a space of time. Huddled on the side of the pitch, every one of the American Samoans was soaked to the skin from the incessant rain. An emotional Rongen spoke to his players. 'I'm so proud of this team,' he said. 'We started together, we finished together. What you can do today is walk off with your heads held high. Be very proud of what you have done for your country. Don't ever forget that. Guys, I won championships with a lot of teams, but

I've got more respect for all of you guys than I've done for most of the teams I've coached. I want to thank you very much for this pretty…' He paused, his eyes welling up with tears, to clear a lump in his throat. '…pretty awesome experience. Let's be proud.'[102]

As frustrating as missing out at the last must have been, perhaps it was for the best. Having exorcised the demons of so long ago and grabbed that first win, the glow of success could now linger a while. To have had to face Oceania's best and had the potential for more heavy defeats may have taken some of the gloss away. This way they could return home with nothing but positivity.

Their exploits in those three matches raised American Samoa eighteen places in the world rankings to an all-time high of 186th. But more than that, it had given a new hope to a team that had for so long been bereft. It had rekindled Thomas Rongen's love for the game and it had given Nicky Salapu his life back.

'After the game I buried everything, whatever happened, like Australia, South Pacific Games,' Salapu commented afterwards. 'I'm going to go back to Seattle [with] no more stress, no more heavy thing on my back. It's like everything… it's all gone,' he added, struggling to adequately describe his feelings of release. Years of frustration and turmoil were washing away. 'I think right now I'm a free man. It feels really good.'[103]

As the players prayed together on the pitch before performing one final *haka*, not of victory, but of redemption, Rongen added: 'It's great for the players, great for soccer in general because it was done by a bunch of amateurs that played the game for love and passion. It was as pure as it can get. I'll carry this with me the rest of my life.'[104]

Worst in the World

Chapter 7: The Ancestral Call

Kenny Dyer knows a thing or two about being up against the odds. As a player and coach of the Montserrat national football team, he had become used to always being the minnow. Belatedly entering the world of international football as a player, he earned the distinction of being the oldest player to take part in the 2010 World Cup qualifiers. He was forty-three years-old when he took to the field in Montserrat's 7-1 defeat to Suriname, their one and only match before their swift, unceremonious elimination. It was also his international debut. But more than that, as the only member of the set up with any professional football experience, he was the player-coach.

'They were a shambles,' he said of his international colleagues on that dispiriting occasion. 'The players who travelled, I wouldn't have picked them for a Ryman's Premier League game. They weren't up to international standard at all… We weren't ready.'[105] A few years later, he made three more appearances for Montserrat in the Caribbean Cup at the age of forty-six, with similar results. If his international playing career was late and limited, it was no less remarkable than the way it had come about.

Dyer is a Londoner, born and bred. As a promising youngster, he'd been a trainee at some of London's bigger clubs, spending time in the youth schemes of Arsenal, Tottenham Hotspur and Charlton Athletic, before finding his natural level a bit lower down the pecking order. Years spent hopping around the non-league clubs of South-East England were interrupted by a couple of spells playing professionally in Cyprus. It was only when his brother took a holiday to Montserrat, where their father had been born, that Dyer's international opportunity came along. His brother made frequent mention whilst in Montserrat of Dyer's professional contract in Cyprus to all who would listen, and this eventually led to a call-up into the national squad and an offer to take charge of the team for the World Cup match against Suriname. 'These opportunities don't come up - it's a once in a lifetime,' he explained. 'It's in my blood. It was a chance for me to try and see what I could do to develop football on the island.'[106]

Dyer was no spring chicken though, and at forty-six, even at the distinctly obscure and lowbrow level of international football that Montserrat inhabited, his playing days were clearly numbered. He continued as coach however, and in keeping with his own recruitment to the national team cause, he set about progressing and enhancing a policy that had begun under his coaching predecessor a few years earlier.

Ruel Fox, once a regular Premier League performer for Norwich, Newcastle, Tottenham and West Bromwich, is without a doubt Montserrat's most famous and successful footballer. Born in Ipswich to Montserratian parents, he was one of the earliest examples of the far flung diaspora making their mark on the national team of their homeland. He played and coached the team through their Caribbean Cup preliminaries in 2004 as a thirty-six year-old, only narrowly losing out to near neighbours, Antigua, 5-4. From him the idea began, later taken up with an additional degree of verve by Dyer, to strengthen the team from the colonial motherland.

Dyer began using his contacts from his years in England's lower reaches to seek out other Montserratians, or players like him with Montserratian heritage, to come and play under the flag of their homeland. As well as numerous families who left the island in the aftermath of the Soufriere Hills volcano eruption, many had fled before and since (as Dyer's family had) for economic reasons and a better life. As Dyer and Montserrat were heading for a date with destiny, kicking off the first of the world's eight hundred and thirty-two qualifying matches for the 2014 World Cup with a preliminary round tie against Belize, his search for players would take him from the public playing fields of North London's Hackney Marshes to Nottingham and Stoke.

* * * * *

Montserrat didn't have much to live up to when it came to performing in the World Cup. Always one of the few who have had to open their campaign when the memories of the previous Finals had barely even begun to fade, they had always been hastily eliminated with minimum fuss. In three qualifying attempts, and just five matches, they managed to concede thirty-three goals while scoring just two. The only mercy of their 7-1 defeat to Suriname in 2010's qualifying campaign was that it was a one-legged tie, so they were spared the kind of repeat beating they had suffered four years earlier. On that occasion, the apparent might of Bermuda sent them packing with 13-0 and 7-0 victories in their two matches.

If a similar fate was to be avoided this time, Dyer would need to find a few gems amongst Montserrat's descendants. For such a tiny country, with clearly restricted population resources, such an approach was not a new one for them; a natural response to both their small population and the loss that was suffered in the wake of the volcanic eruption. 'We have had some unsteady moments here in Montserrat,' said the national team's general manager Claude Hogan in something of an understatement. 'We have lost a huge chunk of our population because of the volcano.'[107]

Amongst the mass exodus of displaced migrants were of course many of Montserrat's footballers. 'Most of our players are over in England as refugees,' said assistant coach, and goalkeeper from 2002's *The Other Final*, Cecil Lake, ahead of the 2010 qualifier. 'We still have a few players left here on the island but most had to leave. We maintain a database though, so we know pretty much where everyone is.'[108] They even had a couple of professional players from England in that 2010 World Cup qualifying defeat to Suriname in Junior Mendes and Wayne Dyer, both playing at Conference level at the time. Wayne Dyer had also played in the 2006 qualifying matches, scoring the country's only goal, their first ever in World Cup qualifying. But the most important thing to those in Montserrat was merely the fact that they could put a team out. As summed up by Claude Hogan: 'It's a victory just to be able to mobilise a team to play in a World Cup qualifier. It means we are still here... Montserrat is still alive.'[109]

What their database of recent migrants couldn't tell them, however, was how many other players living abroad – primarily in England – could qualify for the national team; the second and third generation descendants of early Caribbean migrants. The search for greater numbers and a bit of extra talent took Kenny Dyer back to England and to the playing fields of Hackney Marshes, home to nearly a hundred football pitches and thousands of enthusiastic amateurs of varying levels. In amongst the Sunday leagues and the pub teams, Dyer held an open trial for the world's worst international team.

Several dozen hopeful players turned up, greeted by Dyer's opening speech to identify those eligible for his team.

'I need to know which ones of you has parents, grandparents, great grandparents from Montserrat,' he said to the blankly staring faces in front of him. 'But then one hand raised… and then another… and then another. We managed to assemble the best squad of players that Montserrat ever had,'[110] explained Dyer. The majority of hopefuls were, shall we say, not up to scratch. But in amongst the rough there was the odd gleaming diamond. One of those recruited from the trial was Jaylee Hodgson, a thirty-one year-old striker playing semi-professionally in Leicestershire and filling in his weekends with a bit of extra Sunday League football. He qualified for Montserrat through his grandparents who were born on the island. 'He was a breath of fresh air,' recalled Dyer. 'He was just goals, goals, goals.'[111] With just weeks to go until the World Cup qualifier, Jaylee was on his way into the rarefied world of international football.

Jaylee Hodgson had taken a rather circuitous route to international recognition. As a promising teenager he'd had a trial with Tamworth Town from the higher end of England's non-league. He'd been invited back for a second trial but didn't turn up, his lethargy and misdirected attitude sending his life in another direction. Having grown up in one of England's more deprived estates in Nottingham there were nefarious distractions aplenty. Hodgson gave up on football for several years only to be jarred back into it by personal tragedy. One of the last things his dying cousin had said to him was, 'You should have been a footballer.'[112] This wake-up call took him back to the playing fields and brought countless goals wherever he went around his local amateur leagues. Gradually the level he played at rose, and then came the open trial in Hackney. 'I'd just lost my job too, and two weeks later I was an international footballer,' he said with a chuckle. 'It's funny how things work out.'[113]

Unlike Jaylee, Anthony Griffith had been recruited without the need for a trial. Brought up in Huddersfield, the twenty-four year-old midfield destroyer had carved out a career as a journeyman professional footballer in the lower reaches of the Football League. Playing for Port Vale in England's fourth tier at the time, he jumped at the chance to represent the island of his father. 'My dad died when I was a young boy,' he said. 'So it's an opportunity for me to learn about the history and heritage of where he came from and link up with family members. I'm really looking forward to the challenge of international football.'[114] Prior to his call-up, Griffith had never so much as visited Montserrat, but suddenly he was the star of the show thanks to the fact that he was regularly playing at a level comfortably beyond that of any of his new teammates. 'It's a fantastic opportunity to play international football at any level and I'm delighted to have been called up,' he added.[115]

As well as Jaylee Hodgson and Anthony Griffith, the squad contained several more members of England's lower leagues, and descendants from immigrants now living in the United States and Australia. They were added to a handful of home-grown players for a rather more diversified, and certainly far more experienced, squad than Montserrat had ever been able to muster before. Players weaned on a higher level of football would hopefully bring a superior standard of play to their new national team. 'The atmosphere is first-class among the home-based players and those who've come in from abroad,' Griffith noted. 'I've pictured [the matches with Belize] several times in my head and I'm sure we're going to win.'[116]

Training ahead of the big clashes was limited. One or two training sessions for those based in England ahead of the squad meeting up in Montserrat catered for many of the squad. But it was only once on the island that the full team came together for the first time. For many it was a first trip to the Emerald Isle of their forebears and an opportunity to reconnect with relatives or to revisit their family roots. Montserrat would not host the first leg of the preliminary round match however. Their new stadium in Blakes was, by this time, fully functional, but had failed to make the grade for international matches for the most trivial of reasons. 'It's a shame because we have a pitch that I'd go as far as saying is one of the best in the region,' explained Kenny Dyer. 'But the dressing rooms aren't ready.'[117] For the want of a lick of paint, the "home" leg would have to be played elsewhere. It would take place in the Trinidadian town of Couva. 'Hopefully we can cause a shock and play the next round in front of our own fans,' added Dyer.

On arrival in Trinidad, the team played a few unofficial friendly matches with local club sides as much to allow the team to get to know each other as to fine-tune any preparations for the big match.

'We've got players who work in McDonald's, accountants, a few full-time professionals, policemen,' Kenny Dyer explained to *BBC Radio 5 Live*. 'Some players are seeing each other for the first time. It's about team spirit and camaraderie. We all know where we are and how low-ranked Montserrat is. Playing international football doesn't come to everyone, so the players blessed with the ability will come in and grasp it. It's a big ask, but it's ninety minutes and we can play well.'[118]

'This is the best Montserrat side I've coached,' he added. 'We played in the Caribbean Cup at the end of 2010, and though it didn't go too well for us, we've had several new players come into the side since then from some pretty big leagues. This team is coming along very nicely.'[119] Amidst such a boost in playing standards, it was easy to get a little carried away. 'Our chances are very good. They [Belize] have more experience than us, but we are a quality side.'[120]

* * * * *

The World Cup doesn't begin with all the drawn-out glitz of the opening ceremony in one of the world's grandest cities housing an imposing stadium bursting at the seams with excited onlookers. Far from the bright lights, the speeches, the flags and the ceremony of the opening match of the World Cup finals, the tournament usually opens in surroundings that are rather more austere. Instead of thousands of expectant observers in the stands and billions watching in every corner of the world on television, the opening skirmishes are played out in front of just a handful of people.

For those involved, generally a matter of months after the last World Cup final and years ahead of the one they are aiming for, it is the first step on a lengthy and laborious qualifying process to earn an invite to the big final party. Countries playing their way through opening preliminary rounds in tiny, far flung, exotic locations are almost certain to stumble and fall well before the race for the finals really gets going. Not that the tension, the optimism and the myriad of hopes and dreams being played out are any less firmly-held.

So it was in the less than salubrious surroundings of the Ato Boldon Stadium in Couva on Trinidad's west coast where the 2014 World Cup began in June 2011. A far cry from the glamourous ending that would come more than three years later in Rio de Janeiro's magnificent Maracana, with Messi and Müller, Agüero and Götze. Instead, it began with Jaylee Hodgson and Anthony Griffith and their hastily gathered-together teammates, watched from the dugouts by Kenny Dyer.

Circling the fading athletics track was a collection of distinctly temporary looking stands, filled with rows of blue seats, their colour having waned over the years thanks to the incessant tropical sun. Barely a seat was occupied on this occasion, however, as no more than a few dozen spectators were on hand to witness the opening shots of the greatest show on Earth. Though it was still stiflingly hot, there was no tropical sun beating down on the players as they walked onto the pitch to the accompaniment of the tinny FIFA anthem. Instead it was raining, hard.

Belize were ranked well above their island opponents going into the two-legged clash and made their superiority and greater experience tell with slicker play from the off. Montserrat were still struggling to find their rhythm and some semblance of cohesion when Belize took the lead midway through the first half. By then a nervous Jaylee Hodgson had already been booked following an ambitious overhead kick where he threatened the safety of an opposition defender more than he did the opposition goal. But he and his colleagues gathered themselves and gradually clawed their way back into the contest.

Barely a minute before half-time Hodgson's moment to shine arrived. 'I had a header that went wide of the post, I remember. And then the ball was whipped in, I hit the ball, volley, back of the net.'[121] Montserrat were level and within sight of a shock victory if they could just keep that momentum going. Sadly for them, it was Belize who were reinvigorated by the half-time interval and began the second half in ruthless fashion. Only eight minutes later they were 3-1 up and as the match entered its closing minutes they had extended that to 5-1, Deon McCauley completing a hat-trick by the end.

Hodgson scored a second of his own a few minutes before full-time to add a little more respectability. A 5-2 defeat wasn't quite what they had dreamed of but it was a step up from the unfettered humiliation of previous World Cup campaigns. Their late consolation acted as a dangling carrot ahead of the return match, a glimmer of hope in the driving rain suggesting that there was a slim chance of a fight back. The positive manner in which they'd played gave some measure of belief that this wasn't a completely forlorn hope. 'We had about fifteen chances in the first half of the first game,' Hodgson lamented afterwards. 'We should have buried them.'[122]

'We are very disappointed,' added Kenny Dyer. 'Not so much that we lost, but that we allowed two silly goals in the second half. We are going to have to attack Belize in the return game.'[123] For a short while it seemed that Montserrat may be offered another way past Belize. If there's one thing guaranteed to get FIFA's knickers in a twist it is government interference in a national football governing body. And no sooner had the Belize government informed their national FA that they were "not authorised to represent this country in any local or international competition... on behalf of the Government, people and nation of Belize" and that they would not provide security services for visiting teams and officials than FIFA slapped Belize with a suspension. "Due to the interference of the government of Belize, FIFA cannot take the responsibility of letting the match take place," read the official FIFA verdict.[124]

The match, originally scheduled for a few days after the first leg, was postponed pending a change of heart from the Belize authorities. Had the situation remained, Montserrat would have gone through by default. 'We thought we were going through to the next round and the next stage,' said Kenny Dyer. 'We actually arrived at the hotel in Belize and got the call saying that the game was cancelled. We stayed overnight and went home.'[125]

Days before FIFA's deadline for the resolution of this particular mess, Belize were readmitted and the match had to go ahead, albeit at a neutral venue once more. Playing in Honduras, Montserrat again began promisingly but failed to capitalise. 'We should have been winning 5-0 in the first twenty minutes,' was Dyer's subsequent assessment.[126] As in the first leg, they equalised after Belize had taken the lead, Jaylee Hodgson recording his third World Cup goal. But on this occasion, the fairy-tale ending did not come to pass. There was to be no great fight back and upsetting of the odds. Belize won a comfortable 3-1 in the end, winning 8-3 on aggregate.

Another defeat, yes, but in the context of all that had gone before could it still be considered a success? In terms of winning, clearly not, but it was a significant improvement nonetheless and had provided some of those involved with career highlights in spite of the losses.

Kenny Dyer had put a team together that was far more competitive than the one he initially inherited. The next round of World Cup qualification may have proved a step too far, but perhaps within the more lowly contests between Caribbean cousins, they would have the chance to shine.

For Jaylee Hodgson, the matches with Belize had been a triumph. From the scruffy parks of Leicestershire's amateur leagues to the World Cup was a meteoric leap. But in making that leap he had become one of Montserrat's all-time leading scorers with all three goals in World Cup qualification. 'After I played in the World Cup qualifiers against Belize I went home with all my mementos, my flags and the shirt and all that and my mum said to me: "Don't you remember in 1994 when you said to me and your auntie in the kitchen that you will play in the World Cup?" And I've done it. It is a dream come true.'[127]

Montserrat's challenge would be to continue this promising development into the future. Just a year later the opportunity to do so came with an opening round Caribbean Cup group in which Montserrat would face Suriname, British Virgin Islands and the group's host, Martinique. The squad that had performed so well in the World Cup qualifiers had been supplemented by a handful of additional English-born players. The eighteen-man squad selected by Kenny Dyer contained one or two new faces, and many who had played for Montserrat unofficially in the London-based get-togethers that had become a more frequent and practical means of allowing the squad to practice. 'Some of these players have been with me for seven years,' he explained.

On reaching Montserrat, a few more hastily arranged friendlies gave the chance to bed in the new players. 'We have taken the opportunity to bring the national team here in Montserrat because most people in Montserrat do not know about these players,' said Dyer. 'So we're taken the opportunity to bring them here so they can familiarise themselves with their country, their parent's country, some of them were actually born here but left at an early age.'[128] Even amongst the seriousness of pre-tournament training the search for more players continued. 'A college student from Massachusetts called Alvin Poteen was on holiday in Montserrat, where his father is from, and he saw the national team training and asked if he could join in, so I said yes. It turned out he was a very good central midfielder so he played against Antigua.'[129] That was in an unofficial kick-about with no ranking points on the line sadly; but Montserrat won 2-0. Poteen's impromptu audition was too late to earn him a place in the Caribbean Cup squad, but he had earned his place on the Montserrat FA's database of potential players.

After that successful build up, Dyer's hopes were high when going into the Caribbean Cup games, particularly after the showing against Belize a year before. 'I think this new team is the strongest national team we've ever put together, and I expect positive things from them.'[130] This wasn't the first time such a proclamation had emerged from the Emerald Isle. All such previous claims had seen some improvement in performance but had nonetheless resulted in defeat. Hope sprang eternal, but would it be any different this time around?

A crowd of just 188 in the Stade Georges Gratiant in Martinique saw Montserrat open their Caribbean Cup campaign in August 2012 against Suriname – the same opposition Kenny Dyer had faced in his playing debut five years before. It had been a humbling defeat that day, and history can have an unfortunate habit of repeating itself. Five years on, after all that progress, Montserrat again lost 7-1 to Suriname, trailing from as early as the 3rd minute. Another defeat followed against Martinique, but at least their 5-0 defeat wasn't nearly as bad as what Martinique had inflicted on the British Virgin Islands - they were beaten 16-0. Just a few days later, Montserrat and the British Virgin Islands would clash in their final group fixture. Surely now, at long last, the perfect hapless opposition was in place for Montserrat to finally, belatedly record their first ever official international victory?

An even first 30 minutes belied two teams that, for all their positive talk, were short on confidence and lacked the belief to just go for it. And then, as the first half wore on, the chance to grasp the initiative was presented to Montserrat. Marlon Campbell, one of the new breed of UK-based players, playing his club football with Bethnal Green United, got his international goal scoring record off the mark with two strikes late in the first half to put Montserrat two goals to the good. Minutes later, they were in dreamland when their Australian-based midfielder, Darryl Roach, made it three. Both scorers exemplified the means by which Montserrat's improvement had come about. Both represented the far flung descendants of Montserrat immigrants and both had learned their football in the more stringent environs of minor amateur leagues. While Campbell played in the Essex Senior League for Bethnal Green, Roach had spread his wings a little further and had pitched up in the Victoria State League playing for Port Melbourne Sharks. Between them they had set Montserrat on the path to paradise.

In the second half, Montserrat stuck the knife into their overwhelmed opponents. They almost unbelievably racked up a seven-goal victory of their own for their first win since gaining FIFA recognition. Montserrat's second half scorers were also English-born descendants of immigrants, hardened in England's amateur leagues. Ellis Remy, scorer of a second half brace, boasts a list of clubs in his career that reads like a who's who of South East England's lower leagues. Nineteen defeats and thirteen years after becoming FIFA members – and seventeen years since their last "unofficial" victory - they had finally won a match. They had a little assistance on the way. British Virgin Islands played the last half hour a man down, and the seventh goal was courtesy of a Virgin Islands' own goal, but this was no fortunate backs-to-the-wall smash and grab raid. This was a team ranked as worst in the world handing out the kind of beating that they were more commonly used to receiving.

It had been years in the making, providing vindication for the policies instigated by Ruel Fox and Kenny Dyer. The diaspora had proved their worth and had put a sporting smile on the face of Montserrat. Their progress had been extensive in many ways. 'When I played we didn't have anything, not even towels or shampoo,' recalled Dyer. 'But I've now got us a kit man, physio, goalkeeper coach and so on, and we're making strides.' The search for more recruits and as yet untapped talent goes on unbounded, and with it the aim of continued progress and one day perhaps even a second win. Speaking with the *Guardian* about the ongoing unending search for those eligible to play for Montserrat, Dyer exclaimed: 'Just Google me or the Montserrat FA. We absolutely want to hear from you.'[131]

Worst in the World

Chapter 8: Home Grown

'Defeat is our destiny,' proclaimed Giampaolo Mazza, the former coach of San Marino's national team.[132] He knew what he was talking about. In sixteen years at the helm of the perennial losers of European football, Mazza had presided over eighty-five matches and his team lost all but three of them, often with a staggering number of goals conceded. Two draws and a lone victory in a friendly over Liechtenstein were all he had to show for his years of service – years that had made him the longest serving national team manager in Europe by some margin. Little wonder then that he added that 'the result is not the priority.'[133]

When Giampaolo Mazza decided to call time on his reign in charge at the end of the 2014 World Cup qualifying campaign, San Marino didn't seek to cast the net far and wide in their search for his successor. In spite of years glued to the bottom of the world rankings, years of heavy defeats with little hope or intention to achieve anything more than limiting their losses, they chose again to rely on domestic capability. Without a thought for the potential rewards of enticing some outside proficiency, San Marino looked to promote from within.

When it comes to recruiting the national team coach, there are no restrictions on nationality as there are for players. A new coach can be appointed without the slightest concern for which passport he holds. For the worst teams in the world it can be something of a futile activity to keep relying on their own small pool of football coaches, and many have spurned this option for a better alternative. But that isn't the San Marino way. Mazza was replaced by another local man, Pierangelo Manzaroli, who had been rather successful in coaching the national Under-21 team. 'It's a moment I have always dreamed about,' said the incoming incumbent about his new role. 'It will not be easy to succeed an experienced coach like Mazza. He made a great contribution with his commitment and work ethic. He changed the role of the San Marino coach using a more modern approach.'[134] Manzaroli would be on a hiding to nothing, of course, but at least the only way was up.

Unlike many other doyens of rankings desolation who have trodden the path of importing a little expertise from elsewhere, San Marino have steadfastly stuck to their own for better, or more usually for worse. They have always been coached by a local, and despite their proximity to the footballing behemoth that is Italy, San Marino have consistently shunned the idea of naturalising Italian players with a Sammarinese connection. This is partly for idealistic reasons but also for administrative and legal ones. In a country where it takes ten years for an outsider to qualify for a passport, there are bureaucratic stumbling blocks aplenty preventing such a policy from being implemented. The closeness to Italy does at least allow a Sammarinese coach or player of some potential the opportunity to be involved in a far higher level of football than is available in their homeland, or is available to many in some of the other weakest football countries. They are lucky to be just a few kilometres down the road from a rich, vibrant and very successful football culture.

There have also, over the years, been a handful of Italian Serie A players who have married women from San Marino and expressed an interest in representing their spouse's nation. Their applications for San Marino passports were swiftly rejected. 'Of course, if that was possible, we would do it,' conceded Giorgio Crescentini, president of the San Marino Football Association. 'We cannot take a player from a different state and give him citizenship because the law will not support it,' he explained. 'On the one side I am proud of this special characteristic: we are pure, and perhaps the only ones. This gives us pride.'

Proud they may be, but they are increasingly alone in an ever-changing world. Mass migration as well as the desire of many a footballer to achieve his international ambitions means that the lines of nationality have increasingly overlapped. From Montserrat to American Samoa to East Timor, struggling national teams have frequently sought to supplement their meagre numbers with second and third generation emigrants. UEFA's newest football enclave, Gibraltar, has a population more or less the same as that of San Marino. They too have suffered some heavy qualifying defeats, but in a run of form that must have drawn envious glances from San Marino, Gibraltar have drawn against both Slovakia and Estonia in friendly matches, and beaten Malta. But Gibraltar's squad contained several British players with family connections to the overseas territory, rather than being made up purely of men from the Rock.

Higher up the chain, many countries are only too pleased to snap up foreign-born quality and speed up the passport application process if it will enhance their chances. Some, the likes of Qatar, literally buy in playing quality from other countries, not only in football but across the sporting spectrum. This approach is not for San Marino. Mazza, on leaving his position as national team coach noted: 'The regret is that we never won an official game, but I am proud that we never used a naturalised player.'[135] With this pride comes the acceptance of San Marino's place in European football. 'We are aware of our level and losing is pretty normal for us,' acknowledged Mazza.[136] 'We are weak,' Crescentini concurred. 'But we are pure.'[137]

San Marino's purity is tempered slightly by the presence of several dual-nationals in the team; sons of Sammarinese and Italian parents. Players falling into that category are automatically citizens of the small mountain republic as well as Italy. If they were playing at a high level of professional football then perhaps they would have a choice to make over which nation to represent internationally. For those in the lower and amateur leagues the decision to represent San Marino is a straightforward one. Citizenship of San Marino is a passport into a world that they would never otherwise be a part of. San Marino's players can rub shoulders with the superstars of the game, players they would only normally watch on television competing on the grandest of stages and who play at a level far beyond that of the *Campionato Sammarinese di Calcio* – the national, entirely amateur, top division.

With a population of around 32,000, small enough to fit inside Wembley three times over, the Most Serene Republic of San Marino to give its full title, is a micro-state entirely surrounded by Italy, not far from the Italian city of Rimini. It lays claim to being the world's oldest constitutional republic and despite its diminutive size, is not the smallest country in Europe. It comes in ahead of Monaco and the Vatican City in that particular contest. They don't win out in many other contests though. The corridors of the San Marino Football Association are lined with shelves full of trophies and medals, but none of them are for winning anything internationally.

Having joined FIFA in 1988, San Marino have taken part in every World Cup and European Championship qualifying process since, and are yet to record a competitive victory. With such a small population, their playing resources are naturally rather limited. 'I've got no more than about fifty players to call on,' noted Mazza shortly before his tenure ended. 'Perhaps even a few less.'[138] Given such limited resources, San Marino's record is unsurprising. There have been defeats, heavy defeats and even heavier defeats and a whole heap of criticism along the way. Had San Marino had the good fortune to have been located in the Caribbean or the South Pacific instead of being surrounded by Italy, they may well have had a few regular winnable games over the years and avoided the consistency of their rock bottom ranking.

There have been some dark days, none more so than the 13-0 defeat inflicted by Germany in a European Championship qualifier in late 2006. A twenty-one year-old Lukas Podolski scored four as Germany completed the biggest ever victory in European Championship qualifying. If the humiliation of such a defeat wasn't bad enough, a last minute penalty for the Germans offered the opportunity for the otherwise unemployed German goalkeeper, Jens Lehmann, to get involved. 'Our fans wanted me to shoot [the penalty],' he said afterwards. 'But I thought that it might be considered a humiliation, and the San Marino players were also calling for fair-play, so I went back. It was better that way,'[139] he said. The penalty was scored anyway by the regular taker to complete the rout.

'We had many critics and many people questioning our presence in the group,' recalled Mazza after that defeat, the worst in San Marino's history. The players are, save for a couple of rare exceptions, all amateurs with full-time jobs. There are shop workers, accountants, clerks, factory workers, students, as well as one or two earning a living from the game whether in coaching or playing in Italy's lower leagues. The team have no prima donnas flaunting the wealth and many luxuries that football has brought them. They just have a group of players representing their country with pride, and training in the evenings after work in their spare time.

Just how do they cope with the mental toll of all those defeats, and having to dust themselves off ready to go to work the next day? 'The most important job in San Marino is the psychological state of the players,' Mazza said. 'Our players know we will have negative results so it is important to reconstruct the spirit the day after the game so they can go back to their jobs.'[140] He was constantly preparing his team to try and limit their defeats as much as possible, both to avoid on-field humiliation and to limit the damage to the players' mental state. 'For us the positive remains with the satisfaction of playing famous teams from all around the world,' he continued. 'Usually it's teams we only see on TV and they're pretty famous. We don't feel defeated every time we play with the team; we try and get good results even though we know it's impossible.'[141]

Every time a big European nation is forced to put themselves through the trouble of having to play San Marino, the same calls are repeated: San Marino shouldn't be there, the naysayers will pronounce. They bring nothing to the qualifiers and should have to pre-qualify with all the other hopeless teams that the big boys can't be bothered to play. Needless to say it's not an opinion that is shared in San Marino. 'Sport doesn't cater for things like that,' insisted Mazza, with the passion of a man firmly fighting his corner. 'At the Olympics, champions like Usain Bolt have to go through the heats against less talented athletes. The essence of sport lies in giving everyone the chance to compete. That's what sport's all about.'[142] Certainly within European zone qualifying matches that has always been the case, and it looks likely to remain so for the time being. The strong are drawn alongside the weak and they must face each other.

There is a pre-qualifying precedent in other regions though, where things work differently. The weakest are cast aside before having to face the strongest, but there are often various other factors at play. Greater geographical distances and more complex, and indeed expensive, travel options make including the very weak in a full draw in Asia, Africa or Central America far more difficult. Frequently, some of the weakest in those areas are extremely poor countries, lacking the finances to fund frequent trips all over their continent. Additionally, the gap between the weak and the strong in those areas is generally far greater than it is in Europe, no matter how bad San Marino may appear to the rest of Europe. Like Liechtenstein, Luxembourg, Andorra, just as with Germany, England and Italy, San Marino are members of UEFA and FIFA and an independent nation. As such, they will always be there, coming back time after time; chasing that elusive dream.

113

'Many of the players are non-professional,' said Mirko Palazzi, one of the two professionals in the squad, playing in the Italian fourth division. 'But for one night, we can feel like professionals. That's very, very important. That's why we want to play these matches.'[143]

That 13-0 defeat was the worst moment in their bleak football history, but it was far from an isolated incident. There had been double-digit defeats against Norway, Belgium, Poland and the Netherlands over the years as well as countless concessions of five, six, seven and eight. Precious few goals had been scored at the other end. San Marino's all-time top goal scorer, Andy Selva, has scored just eight times. Even with that meagre total, he is streets ahead in the national scoring charts. Next best is Manuel Marani with two goals, and ten others have scored a single goal each. And that is it.

When dealing in defeat – sustained, never-ending defeat – it pays to draw highlights from other means. As lowly as San Marino have always been in European football's echelon they have had their occasional moments in the sun. None more so than the day they added to the embarrassment and humiliation of the hapless England of Graham Taylor. Even in that numerically limited tally of goal scorers, one player made a significant mark on world football with his lone strike for San Marino. Davide Gualtieri, a twenty-two year-old computer salesman, secured his place in football history when he scored against England after only 8.3 seconds of their World Cup qualifier in late 1993, still to this day the fastest goal in World Cup history. His strike became one of the defining images of England's morose demeanour under Taylor (although England ultimately won 7-1), and ensured his place in San Marino's sporting folklore with hero status in the mountain-top nation. It gained him international renown too. 'Even now, some fans from around the world are always coming into my shop with pictures of me and shirts for me to sign,' he revealed in one of his many interviews with the English press ahead of another clash with England in 2013.[144]

When the most supreme moment in a nation's football past is the scoring of a single goal in a 7-1 defeat, it is clear the nation in question is no sporting giant. Success of any sort will always be hard to come by, with the long hard slog of defeat after defeat being punctuated only by the occasional moment of joy. Gualtieri's goal, came after a disastrously under hit back pass by Stuart Pearce straight from the kick-off, and far overshadowed all seven of the English goals which followed. 'I remember we kicked off and we lost the ball, but I kept running anyway,' recalled Gualtieri. 'Then Pearce hit the ball too softly and I was ready. It was not the best goal I ever scored, but it was the most beautiful.'[145]

England had gone into the match, played in an eerie and almost empty stadium in nearby Bologna, knowing that they needed to win by seven clear goals to have any hope of reaching the 1994 World Cup, and even then they were relying on Holland failing to beat Poland in the group's other match. Thanks to Gualtieri, they missed their target by one, although the Dutch result (they won 3-1) made England's last-ditch attempt to qualify ultimately futile in any case. But at the time he scored it, England's hopes had been still alive. England's players were so numbed by the shock of conceding so early and so disastrously that it took them fully twenty-two minutes to draw level. 'To score such a famous goal was unthinkable,' Gualtieri recalled years later. 'I still laugh about it now. I remember the surprise on everybody's face. Nobody believed San Marino could score against mighty England, certainly not after eight seconds. When I see the goal now, I still wonder how we managed to score straight from the kick-off against one of the biggest teams in football.'[146]

He wasn't the only one to wonder just how it had happened. Sat in the England dugout, the beleaguered and soon to be unemployed England coach Graham Taylor felt his world crumbling around him. 'It was the only time in my whole life when I closed my eyes, looked up to the sky and asked, "What have I done wrong?"', admitted Taylor some years afterwards. 'On a night when we needed everything to go our way, I couldn't believe it – and I don't think the San Marino forward could believe his luck either.' Taylor was certainly correct there. For Gualtieri, having missed out on the reverse fixture at Wembley through illness, simply being on the same pitch as England's high profile stars was a dream come true. Scoring was in another realm altogether. 'To score such a famous goal is unthinkable – it is like winning the World Cup,' he said.[147]

A brutal English media laid into its team and head coach showing no mercy. The headline "End of the World" in the *Mirror* summed up the prevailing feeling rather well. Gualtieri commented that the San

Marino players didn't really speak to any of their English counterparts because 'they were all a bit angry'. He has a DVD of the match which has had several viewings over the years. 'Sometimes if I'm feeling a bit down, I'll play it again just to cheer myself up,' he said. 'It always works.'[148]

'After the game, I exchanged shirts with Pearce,' Gualtieri recalled. 'I have other shirts I swapped with opponents, but of course that one from Pearce is my favourite. I keep it safe at home. It makes me smile when I look at it and it makes me laugh when I think about the goal I scored.'[149] A single goal it may have been, but it affected more than just San Marino. 'What I did,' he remembered fondly years later, 'changed the events of qualification.'[150]

Also in the San Marino team that day was Massimo Bonini; without question San Marino's greatest ever player. In a glittering career in the top reaches of Italian football, he spent six seasons with the mighty Juventus, winning several league titles and a host of other trophies including a European Cup in the ill-fated 1985 final against Liverpool. Prior to San Marino's inclusion into UEFA and FIFA, players from San Marino could opt to switch nationality and play for Italy. Bonini played for the Italian Under-21 team in his youth, but his refusal to give up his citizenship of San Marino meant that until San Marino were accepted into the global football fold, he missed out on full international honours. He was thirty-one when he was able to make his belated debut for his homeland. In all his nineteen caps, he tasted nothing but defeat, having missed out through injury on the 0-0 draw with Turkey in the same World Cup campaign that saw Gualtieri grab his moment of fame.

That point against Turkey had only been added to, competitively, by a 1-1 draw with Latvia eight years later; a result which prompted the Latvian coach Gary Johnson to resign immediately afterwards in humiliation. Otherwise, it was all defeat. In friendly matches they had once, just once, gone one better. One particular day in 2004 will live long in the memory of all involved for it was the day San Marino recorded their only ever win; 1-0 over Liechtenstein. The scorer that day, and still the only man to have ever scored a winning goal for San Marino, was their all-time top scorer Andy Selva.

Still in the national squad at the start of the Euro 2016 qualifying campaign as a thirty-eight year-old, Selva had a glorious past by San

Marino standards. His international career had begun with something of a bang, scoring on only his second appearance for the national team as a fresh twenty-two year-old. Born to an Italian father and a Sammarinese mother, he was a citizen of both and as such he qualified to represent either. As a young professional player making his way in the second and third tiers of Italian football, the reality was that the chance of representing the Italian *Azzurri* was remote. But his Sammarinese nationality afforded him his international opportunity, and he grasped it.

'I've had the chance to play against great defenders like Carles Puyol – he was from another planet, simply amazing,' Selva said, reliving his most memorable encounters. 'Andrea Pirlo and Raul, they are great guys and real champions too. They gave us a lot of compliments after the games, even though the difference between our team and theirs is huge.'[151]

If Selva had burst onto the scene as a young man, scoring so early in his international career, then his peak period came a few years later. Remarkably, for a San Marino striker, he scored three goals in four international appearances in a brief spell from June 2004, the first of which was the only goal in that lone win over Liechtenstein. 'It is a great memory for me,' he recalled. 'I remember my teammates embracing me. It is something we all felt on the pitch. After the final whistle you start thinking: "What have I done? I have made something historical."'[152] That was at a time when his club career was at its height, playing for the likes of Padova, Sassuolo and Hellas Verona, though he would never reach the hallowed ground of Italy's top division. In a career of international highs and lows, Selva described playing at Wembley as 'a dream' but was accepting of San Marino's place in football hierarchy. 'Our challenge is to improve in each game and to learn with each hard defeat and that is the nature of playing for San Marino and how our life has been in football.'[153]

Selva hit the back of the net in narrow losses to Belgium and Wales during a period that was arguably San Marino's finest. There was the win over Liechtenstein of course, but scattered sporadically amongst the near endless stream of heavy losses there was the occasional near miss, when a more favourable twist of fate, here or there, could have given San Marino some truly memorable moments. The likes of Wales and Ireland have almost come a cropper in San Marino, only to escape with the victory, if not their pride, at the last moment. Ireland in particular were exceptionally fortunate to have avoided the embarrassment of failing to beat San Marino.

With just three minutes left on the clock Ireland were 1-0 up but a terrible defensive mix-up between Irish goalkeeper Wayne Henderson and his centre backs allowed midfielder Michele Marani to gleefully roll the loose ball into the now unguarded Irish net. A comedy goal, but far from a laughing matter for the Irish who were now staring down the barrel of their most humiliating result. San Marino hunkered down in an effort to see out the scarcely believable draw. They made it to ninety minutes. They made it to ninety-four minutes. But in the fifth minute of added time, in fact just eight seconds from the end of the allotted five extra minutes, a desperate last gasp corner led to a scramble in the crowded penalty area from which Stephen Ireland ruined what would have been a dramatic tale of underdog bite, and poked home a late, late winner.

He may have spared Irish blushes but it also devastated the now distraught San Marino players, who fell to the ground in exhausted anguish. To have come so painfully close to a competitive draw against a team ranked as highly as Ireland was a bitter pill to swallow. Eight seconds. Eight short lonely seconds from the most famous result in their history. Most reports of the match naturally focused on the failings and shortcoming of the Irish: spared blushes, complaints of complacency, and a general wailing at the ineptitude of the Irish manager at the time was the order of the day. But from the perspective of the little man, having taken on a giant and oh-so-nearly slain them, it was equally as painful in a wholly different way.

* * * * *

'I will take the job with great enthusiasm,' said Pierangelo Manzaroli, San Marino's new man at the helm. 'The same enthusiasm I want to see in my players because when they enter the pitch they are representing San Marino.'[154] In an unusual turn of events for San Marino, when Manzaroli took over from Giampaolo Mazza following the end of the 2014 World Cup qualifying campaign he brought with him a smidgen of an international track record. In four years coaching the national under-21 side, he had achieved the seemingly impossible in winning a competitive match – 1-0 over Wales – the first competitive victory for a San Marino team at any level. They had also managed goalless draws with Finland and Greece. Not much by most country's standards admittedly, but for San Marino this was an unprecedented level of attainment. Could Manzaroli translate this junior level success into an improvement in the fortunes of the senior national team?

Manzaroli's approach was subtly different to that of his predecessor. Previously the aim had always been to limit the losses as much as possible. Battening down the hatches and crowding the defence was often the only tactic. Against the very best that would still be the case, but when up against teams a notch or two below the real heights of the European game, though still well above San Marino's calibre, the approach was now slightly different.

'Mine is a tenacious team who has a great desire to do well and who always start with the mindset of winning any game,' he announced rather optimistically ahead of a match with England in late 2014. 'When I prepare for these important games I talk to my players, try to convey confidence and establish a winning mentality. Games always start from 0-0.' He was full of praise for his squad and the attitude they displayed in the face of repeated defeat and international criticism. 'I'm lucky to coach guys who always want to improve, game after game, without thinking too much about the defeats. We're getting closer to a vision of football that is more and more professional. You must remember, however, that our players play in amateur leagues, training only in the evening.'[155]

His arrival must have been a breath of fresh air to the battered squad. Not that their desire and attitude was anything other than professional and aspirational under Mazza, far from it. But a change of leader and a gentle change in outlook was surely a refreshing switch. Locked into their endless cycle of defeat, the arrival of a new coach who many of them had worked with successfully in the under-21 side would herald a renewed level of hope.

'Obviously there is a great difference between the under-21s and the senior team, but not in terms of the approach to games that is needed,' he added. 'I think this is what has allowed San Marino teams to improve in recent years. The last two years have shown that football in San Marino is alive, we just have to stay on this path and continue to give greater importance to small details in our work.'[156] The impending Euro 2016 qualifying campaign would provide the evidence of whether or not Manzaroli's San Marino could alter the course of their fortunes in any way, or continue as they had done before. 'You never know when the chance will arrive to get a result,' he noted, with more than a hint of optimism.[157]

The Manzaroli era had begun inauspiciously though, losing 3-0 in a friendly clash with Albania but it was in the competitive arena of the European qualifying matches where any improvement would really be judged. It began with a narrow 2-0 loss to Lithuania that in reality could have been more but for the saves of Aldo Simoncini in goal. More defeats, albeit expected ones, followed against England and Switzerland but the margin of those defeats suggested that not much had changed for San Marino. However, the team had been set up and had played in an ever-so-slightly more progressive manner than before. With Mazza in charge they had become increasingly well-practiced in the ultra-defensive approach, playing with little or no ambition in attack. Under Manzaroli, the approach was gradually more positive.

What began rather tentatively against Lithuania, where they only managed a significant effort on goal in the dying minutes, had become altogether more adventurous by the time Switzerland visited Serravalle. Nothing exemplified this more than a marauding run forwards from San Marino's right-back, Giovanni Bonini, in the opening seconds. He surged into the Swiss penalty area and latched onto a neat diagonal pass from the midfielder Alex Gasperoni. His effort on goal was saved by the Swiss goalkeeper, but such ambition from the off, and from a defender no less, was startling. Their attacks were sporadic throughout, but they were at least attempting something positive. They lost the game, as they were always likely to against that pedigree of opposition, but it signified a step in the right direction in terms of their approach at least. Next up would be Estonia at home a month later in November 2014.

* * * * *

In the driving rain of a dark, dank and sodden evening, San Marino's players took to the field in their distinctly provincial-looking national stadium facing, as they always do, a far higher-ranked opponent. Estonia had beaten Norway just days before and were in buoyant mood. In the sparsely populated stands that surround the grandly titled *Stadio Olimpico,* the scattered groups of supporters, fully exposed to the incessant elements, sought shelter under their flags and banners. Most of the spectators were there to support just one of the teams: the visiting Estonians. Local optimism from the Sammarinese towards their luckless team was in short supply and those who had travelled south from the Baltic had done so in full expectation of victory. The atmosphere, as damp as the autumnal air, was suitably soporific as all present knew what they expected to happen - the same thing that had happened on each of the previous seventy times San Marino had played.

As the action unfolded with the ball skidding quickly off the damp surface, chances were, unusually, not appearing at just one end of the pitch. Remarkably, the men from the micro-state were asserting themselves all over the pitch and pushing forwards when the opportunity arose. It wasn't all out attack of course, far from it – they were up against vastly superior opposition after all – but it was a sign of further improvement and a signal to their few fans that they wouldn't go down without a fight. There were still numerous Estonian efforts on goal to repel, but as the game progressed from first half to second and the night got still darker and wetter, the score-line remained blank.

The San Marino squad was the usual mixture of shop workers, bank clerks, factory workers and students, with the occasional lawyer and olive oil salesman thrown in. A couple of lower league professionals improved the overall standard a little, and in the now thirty-eight year-old striker Andy Selva there was an ex-professional who had become a football coach. He was enjoying an atypical amount of attacking possession and opportunity; a rare luxury in this team. At the other end of the pitch from him was the part-time player, and full-time accountant, Aldo Simoncini: the last line of defence and guarder of their goal.

As a man used to conceding goals in great numbers, it could be claimed his training as an accountant was the perfect grounding for his other career as San Marino's goalkeeper. But there is more to the story of the twenty-eight year-old semi-professional than merely being the hapless and frequently beaten man between the San Marino sticks. As a highly rated teenager, he had played for Modena in Italy's Serie B, the same level reached by Andy Selva and one that only the great Massimo Bonini had exceeded as a Sammarinese. Instead of fulfilling his dreams and becoming a fully-fledged professional, however, his path took a different turn. His aspirations were curtailed by a terrible car accident in 2005 after which he was unsure of even playing the game again, let alone climbing to a higher level. He had shattered his left pelvis and elbow, and spent many months in hospital recuperating. At the time, the doctors weren't even sure he'd be able to walk normally again.

'My life was in danger. I was told I might not be able to play football ever again,' he later recalled in a *BBC* interview. Any chance of a top level career was gone. 'I spent five-six months in bed without moving. When I first got up, I had no muscles left at all. I had lost eight, nine kilograms of muscle mass. It was a very difficult moment.'[158]

He fought back from that adversity. 'When I finally got out of bed, I worked hard to recover,' he said. 'In the summer of 2006 I started with my first training session. Nothing too serious. Just to get the feeling a bit.'[159] Barely a few months later, and a year and a half after the accident, he took his place in the San Marino goal for the first time at the raw age of nineteen. For a man so young, so inexperienced and so physically fragile, to be making an international debut was difficult enough. But for Simoncini, the task was made all the more difficult given the opposition for that Euro 2008 qualifier in September 2006. It was only the (at the time) three time World Champions and recent World Cup semi-finalists Germany. 'We lost 13-0 but that didn't matter to us.' Simoncini was just thrilled to be playing and representing his country. 'Even though I had to pick the ball out of the net thirteen times, it was one of the happiest moments of my life. I put behind me eighteen months of agony. After being told I might not play again, to be part of such a game was simply unforgettable.'[160]

In spite of his long term injury lay off he did still make some inroads towards the professional game in Italy without ever quite reaching the promised land. He made it onto Serie A side Cesena's books for the 2011/12 season though he was only their third choice goalkeeper and never took the field in the big league. And yet at international level he has come face to face with some of the biggest names in the sport. As neatly described by one online article: "He's come into contact with a world that doesn't belong to him."[161] But it's a world that excites him and one he relishes having even brief contact with. 'To play against the biggest players in the world is fascinating. We are amateurs yet we have the opportunity to meet the best players in the world, it's fantastic.'[162] As if to emphasise the chasm between the world inhabited by Simoncini and that of his vaunted opponents, he once chose to miss a qualifying match in Ukraine in order to study for an impending accountancy exam.

It's an odd feeling for a footballer to go into most matches certain of the outcome, and not in a good way. It requires a certain attitude and strength of character that San Marino's players have learned to develop over the years. For Simoncini, in particular, as the goalkeeper picking the ball out his net time and time again, that strength of character must by necessity be even more marked. As the man himself said, 'A San Marino player must have a lot of heart and be willing to suffer.'

'We are aware of the difference between our team and our opponents,' he added. 'But we never take the field to lose. What is crucial is not to let yourself down when you concede the first goal. You have to maintain the nil-nil as long as you can. A beautiful save can cheer you up."[163] In his years in goal for the worst team in the world, he has made plenty of saves to provide him with some brief cheer. Like Nicky Salapu for American Samoa, the goalkeepers for the weakest teams get a lot of practice. They are beaten many times but it would be so much worse without their numerous saves. And yet, it must ultimately be slightly soul-destroying seeing your best efforts at stemming an onrushing tide frequently come to nought. 'I get frustrated from time to time,' Simoncini admitted. 'Nobody wants to lose in football, even less by big scores. But we know very well that some opponents are simply out of reach for us. Let's be honest here, losing by six, seven, eight goals isn't pleasing for anyone. Not even for me. When I notice that the others go four times faster than us, it pisses me off.'[164]

Other than being on the receiving end of regular heavy defeats, Simoncini has claimed another unwanted record in his spell in international football (still related to goals conceded, naturally). Along with his twin brother Davide, Aldo Simoncini is part of the only brother combo to have both scored an own goal in the same international match. This deed of particular notoriety came against Sweden in 2010, another in the long line of bruising losses.

'A professional player wouldn't be able to tolerate a series of similar defeats – he would surely collapse,' said Simoncini of the mental toll of life at the bottom. 'I live it all like it's a dream, and I put all my effort into it; for me it's a privilege, and all the matches I've played have been a great life experience for me.'[165] That is a feeling sometimes enhanced by his illustrious opponents. Of England, a regular opponent in recent campaigns, Simoncini commented, 'They are real gentlemen and they made us feel like we were on the same level.' And even that big moody genius Zlatan Ibrahimovic was similarly encouraging. Simoncini recalled an incident from another clash with Sweden: 'One of my teammates asked him to avoid pounding us because we were playing poorly. He said, "Don't you dare see it that way, just focus on giving it your best shot." We lost 5-0, but at the end of the match Zlatan came over to congratulate me.'[166]

In his forty-one appearances for the national team, Simoncini had known nothing but defeat. He'd been a part of teams that had come close, but had experienced neither victory nor parity in international football. With only minutes remaining of the clash with Estonia it was still goalless, and at long last an unlikely opportunity had presented itself. San Marino stood on the brink of history. The last twenty minutes had seen many chances come and go, but stunningly many of them were for San Marino. They couldn't quite find the breakthrough that would have nudged them in front and into delirium, but they were a threat – time and time again. But as the minutes ticked by, the nerves began to jangle. Estonia had forced many a save from Simoncini in the San Marino goal and their threat was ever present.

Moments from an unforgettable result, any Sammarinese desire to push on in search of a winner was tempered by the more pragmatic view of holding on to what they had. The increasingly desperate Estonian forwards piled forwards in an effort to spare the blushes they could surely already feel beginning to envelop them and forced two excellent late chances, both falling to their veteran striker Ingermar Teever. The first was missed from dangerously close in on goal, hit high and away when a more composed finish would surely have won it for Estonia. Then in injury time, he met a corner with a towering header while the San Marino defenders stood statuesque with petrified paralysis. The header glanced wide, leaving the visiting players clutching their heads in despair and the home team breathing huge sighs of relief.

As the final whistle blew moments later, the soaked San Marino players, to a man a study in expressions of disbelief, suddenly found previously hidden energy reserves as the celebrations began. The man they all ran towards, the man who had done more than any other to achieve this modest success, was stood in his goalmouth with his arms aloft and his face raised to the night sky above. It was as though the driving rain was washing away all that had gone before. all those beatings, all those goals conceded, all that pain and humiliation. Aldo Simoncini had made a string of fine saves throughout the game to keep the Estonians at bay and claim only San Marino's third ever clean sheet. Simoncini had become a national hero. It was a step into the unknown but was, he noted, 'an incredible feeling.'

The result, if not quite sending shockwaves around the world, did at least cause a ripple. The world's media rolled out stunned headlines making great use of capital letters: "San Marino DON'T lose" in the *Daily Mail*, or "San Marino claim FIRST EVER qualifying point" in the *Mirror*. *La Gazzetta dello Sport*, the Italian sports newspaper hailed the result as having finally earned "1 Real Point", while the local San Marino *Libertas* declared "Draw! Missing since 1993 in the San Marino home".

It was only a 0-0 draw but it earned San Marino sufficient ranking points to lift them well clear of the bottom of the FIFA table. That single result, coming against a team ranked no less than one hundred and twenty places higher than them, and coming in a competitive regional qualifier in the strong UEFA confederation rather than in a friendly match, saw San Marino's ranking points tally rocket from a stone cold zero up to a frankly startling fifty-five. This newly-acquired total was enough to see them climb twenty-eight places in the rankings taking them up to joint-180th alongside such greats of the game as Bermuda and Cambodia. Not only that, but they were no longer the worst team in Europe having leapfrogged Andorra, another nation similarly reliant on domestic coaching expertise.

San Marino had been stuck at the foot of FIFA's rankings for a depressingly long time, seeing the likes of Montserrat, the Turks & Caicos Islands, Guam and American Samoa come and go from the worst in the world club they had cohabited from time to time. Now it was San Marino's turn to leave their lowly ranking behind, all thanks to that improbable draw.

'In recent months our workload has increased and the work has paid off,' said Pierangelo Manzaroli. 'This result is a reward for the players and it will be an incentive to gain other good results sooner than in twelve years' time.'[167] Harking back to their lone win all that time before, the feelings were different this time. This result, though not a win, was on an entirely different level: a better opponent, a competitive point and a renewed, or perhaps more appropriately newborn, sense of optimism. It may well prove little more than another freak result – a flash in the pan – before they regress to their mean once more and start another long line of defeats. But none of that would take away from what they had achieved and the feelings it had invoked.

'I remember the win in Liechtenstein but this has a different meaning,' said Andy Selva, the only remaining link to the team from that long-past day. 'I have been waiting for a result like this for eleven years... We searched for this result for years and now we found it.'[168]

Chapter 9: The Generosity of the British Virgin Islands

Could there be a football tournament in the world that sounds more enticing to the casual observer than the Caribbean Cup? The thought of warm, inviting turquoise seas, pristine white sands, lush green islands, cool music and an all-round laid-back atmosphere with the added bonus of tournament football is a tantalising one. For some of the world's worst football teams it also provides a priceless opportunity to play against their peers; contests between weak, sparsely populated island nations that offer a rare chance of victory.

More frequently in their usual fixtures, the Caribbean contingent of the "worst in the world" gets pitched against someone higher up the scale on the sporadic occasions they take to the field. Countries, or rather territories, as exotically named as the Turks and Caicos Islands, the US Virgin Islands, and of course Montserrat, struggle valiantly against those with far greater resources than themselves and are generally unable to cope. In World Cup qualification, for instance, those at the bottom of the CONCACAF federation, to which the Caribbean nations belong, face a two-legged play-off against a superior team. In the normal course of events, they are summarily dismissed at this stage by a troublesome margin, before slinking off into the background from whence they came. Years can sometimes roll past before there is a return to action and a repeat of the process.

But, amongst that oft-repeated cycle of difficulty, the biennial Caribbean Cup provides a setting for some of the smallest nations on earth to battle each other in a series of more egalitarian contests. In short, it provides the prospect of victory. Not victory in the overall tournament of course; that would be taking things too far! Even in the membership of the Caribbean Football Union – a subsidiary of CONCACAF – there is a gang of stronger nations that feed ruthlessly on the weak. They may not be much in world terms, but Trinidad & Tobago, Jamaica, Haiti and Cuba not only have a wealth of people to choose from compared to many of their Caribbean colleagues, but also have a thriving popularity for the game and football heritage of sorts. All four have qualified in the past for the World Cup Finals.

But in the Windward Islands and the Leeward Islands, dotted amongst the larger land masses, there are sufficient diminutive nations as to make the Caribbean Cup qualifiers a more even contest for the particularly weak. No Caribbean nation has done as much to assist their neighbours in this regard than the British Virgin Islands. For a team that has never sunk to the very bottom of the rankings themselves, the British Virgin Islands have had a considerable effect on those that have. It has become something of a recurring theme in the Caribbean that if you are truly desperate for a result to gain a few ranking points, it would be of real benefit to have a fixture against the British Virgin Islands on your schedule.

This may seem rather harsh on the sun-smacked collection of tax havens that make up the British Virgin Islands. After all, they have never been a part of the worst in the world club even for a single month. They have come perilously close on one or two occasions however – their lowest ranking being 203rd in mid-2014 – but have stayed clear by familiar means. Victories were few and far between, but those they did achieve were generally against even smaller islands: the likes of Anguilla and Montserrat. As a result, the British Virgin Islands have, until now, always found a way of keeping their heads sufficiently above water so as to avoid any chance of drowning. This is in contrast to many of their near neighbours who have repeatedly floundered, in some cases for lengthy periods of time. We have already seen how Montserrat's protracted stay in the worst in the world fellowship was finally, gloriously ended with a resounding and remarkable 7-0 win over the British Virgin Islands, but they are not alone.

Near neighbours, the US Virgin Islands, ended their own lengthy spell at the bottom of the rankings thanks to two drawn friendly local derbies – "Battles of the Virgins", if you will. Days later, they contrived to lose a World Cup qualifier 10-0 to Grenada, but had risen from their ranking low point thanks to the draws with their neighbours. By the time of the next World Cup cycle, the two Virgin Islands teams were drawn to face each other in the preliminary round playoffs. 'It has that local derby feel,' said US Virgin Islands midfielder Reid Klopp. 'They're so close. They're right there over the water.'[169] Klopp would score in both legs of the playoff as the US Virgin Islands continued their slow but steady rise up the rankings and secured a place in the first group stage of World Cup qualifying for the very first time.

* * * * *

'Your Country Needs You!' proclaimed the headline on the website of the national football association. 'If you originate from the Turks & Caicos Islands and are playing soccer overseas you could be eligible to represent the Turks & Caicos Islands in the 2006 World Cup Qualifiers.'[170] This digital appeal bore fruit. Amongst no doubt hundreds of hopefuls rapidly checking the birth certificates of their parents and grandparents, eager to fulfil their World Cup dreams, there were a few genuine contenders. Gavin Glinton, then of the Major League Soccer side Dallas Burn, and his brother Duane who played at a slightly lower level, were both recruited as were a few amateur players from England. Gavin Glinton was the prize however; the real jewel in the crown. He would play for several years in America's top professional league.

Having only been formed in 1996 by British expats, and becoming affiliated to FIFA two years later, the Turks and Caicos Islands Football Association was a somewhat primitive operation. Indeed football comes well behind basketball in terms of popularity on the islands. It comes well behind dominoes too for that matter. Without a pitch, players, or a national league to call their own, it was a football association in name more than anything else, initially. With resources limited on all fronts, and finances almost non-existent, they had to turn to FIFA grants to supplement their own fundraising in order to subsidise the setup of their infrastructure. That bought them a proper international standard pitch complete with floodlights.

With their newfound facilities under construction, an early excursion into the Caribbean Cup saw the Turks and Caicos Islands record their first official draw, holding the US Virgin Islands to a 2-2 draw the year after their FIFA membership was obtained. But FIFA's eyes were focused more on their global tournament, and their money didn't come for free. In return for financial assistance, the Turks and Caicos Islands were obliged to remain active with international fixtures, and most importantly to enter and take part in the World Cup qualifiers, ready or not.

129

Their first venture into this previously unknown world didn't go well. The hardly giant St Kitts & Nevis sent them packing at the first hurdle of the 2002 tournament qualifiers, 14-0 on aggregate. That experience left them minded to put their minimal finances to more productive use when the time came for the 2006 qualifiers. Why waste precious money on the logistics and expense of hosting one match and travelling for another when the outcome was seemingly assured from the outset? With heavy defeat certain, they felt their money would be better spent on development programmes, youth coaching, training camps and the like – laudable attempts to improve their overall standard. Money was still so scarce that on occasion green paint was used to cover bare patches on the pitch as it was cheaper than continually watering the grass. 'The idea to put out a national team was barmy,' said Chris Gannon, a centre-back on the national team who doubled as the country's fire chief. 'It would have been far better to invest in five-a-side pitches for kids.'[171] But FIFA felt differently.

A letter arrived from FIFA headquarters demanding that the Turks and Caicos Islands enter a team into the qualifiers or face losing their financial assistance. With little option but to comply, the players held raffles to finance travel to away matches and the national FA sought to supplement their meagre playing numbers. That led to the website appeal and to Gavin and Duane Glinton.

'Their appearances were the biggest bonus to our national development,' said Gannon. 'The kids in this country now have two genuine sporting heroes to emulate instead of a bunch of ageing white fellas puffing their way round the pitch... I cannot speak highly enough about what they have done for our little country.'[172]

As much as the Glintons may have raised the quality of the Turks and Caicos squad and boosted the aspirations of local kids, on the field – in the pressure-cooker of the World Cup qualifiers – their effect wasn't enough to secure a victory. Drawn to face the regional might of Haiti, the islanders again lost both matches, played in neutral Miami, but by narrower margins than had been the case in the previous World Cup. Having lost the first match 5-0, they held their superior opponents to only a two-goal victory in the second match, even going close to scoring in a goalless second half.

This progress continued into the subsequent Caribbean Cup campaign a couple of years later. They surpassed all they had achieved before to record their first ever victory – 2-0 over the Cayman Islands – before narrowly losing out to the Bahamas. Eighteen months later, they fared even better when the next batch of World Cup qualifiers came round again. A 2-1 home win over St Lucia was a maiden victory in the World Cup, though the concession of a stoppage-time goal made their first leg advantage more slender than it need have been. 'There were at least 2,000 people there,' said the national FA chief. 'Which when you think of it in proportional terms is the equivalent of about three million people turning up to watch an England game.'[173] The team celebrated the win afterwards in a nearby beach bar along with most of the 2,000 spectators. Confidence was high, but was sadly misplaced. St Lucia duly won the second leg 2-0 to eliminate the Turks and Caicos. But that was the high point. As the finances dwindled away once more, and the player pool remained steadfastly limited, the Turks and Caicos Islands drifted gradually but inexorably towards the bottom of the world rankings. Inevitability the downward pull proved too strong and they eventually succumbed to hitting rock bottom in early 2012.

* * * * *

'I did once take a pub side in Hull to a Sunday League title,' said Matthew Green, the English expat and Technical Director of the Turks and Caicos Islands Football Association. 'But that was a bit different to running an international team.'[174] Green is responsible for overseeing football development on the islands, as well as having had a stint as coach of the national team. Quite the rise for the former youth trainee at Hull City who went on to become a teacher after being released by his home town club as a fifteen year-old.

His teaching career took him from Humberside to the Bahamas. 'I had a friend who worked in the Bahamas and my plan was to go visit him on vacation and see if I could find work while I was there,' he explained. 'I got a teaching job in a school and when I found out that they didn't have a soccer programme I put one in place. It was very popular.' It was very successful too. He coached the high school girls' team to seven consecutive national titles. 'From there I worked my way up, going through various coaching academies and eventually becoming director of women's football in the Bahamas.'[175]

Then, in late 2006, he spotted an advert for the Technical Director job in Turks and Caicos and decided to give it a go. 'I'm loving it,' he said, as though scarcely able to believe his luck in where he ended up. 'There's something different for me to do every day. I manage the men's and women's teams, and on a non-match day I could be doing anything from watching other matches, assessing referees, organising regional academies, to washing kit.'[176]

'Within a few years we have managed to put together a pretty strong youth programme and our grassroots programme is pretty big,' he added after six years in the role. 'We now have over twenty leagues and competitions across all ages and sexes. A few years ago we had three.'[177] This progress behind the scenes was certainly impressive but when it came to the senior national team, positive results were as scarce as ever. Now several years on from the progress made in the narrower World Cup qualifying defeats to Haiti and the wins over the Cayman Islands and St Lucia, the Turks and Caicos Islands were the worst in the world, having long forgotten what it felt like to win a match.

Gavin Glinton was still around and still playing professionally, though his career, now very much winding down, had taken him from the glamour of the United States and the MLS to the Vietnamese Second Division and a club called Mikado Nam Dinhis. Getting him back to the islands for training camps or matches was a logistical and financial nightmare, as it was for some of their more talented youngsters on scholarships in the United States or England. Against this backdrop, the qualifiers for the 2014 World Cup saw Matthew Green coaching the team to a 10-0 aggregate loss to the Bahamas and instant elimination. Those defeats were the one to complete the slide to the worst in the world and saw the team go into international hibernation for almost three years. When they belatedly returned to action, it was for the preliminary qualifying round of the 2014 Caribbean Cup where they would face Aruba, French Guiana and the British Virgin Islands.

* * * * *

Amid the ornate and vividly coloured gingerbread-house old colonial architecture of Oranjestad – the capital city of Aruba in the southern Caribbean – and far from the luxurious resorts pampering many an American honeymooner, sits the unassuming Guillermo Prospero

132

Trinidad Stadium. From the outside, Aruba's national stadium resembles little more than a brightly painted office building; a colourful delight of yellow and azure blue, with a pink roof topping it off. On the inside, long yellow benches which have clearly seen better days flank the artificial pitch in the small main stand. Each end of the stadium is little more than a curved yellow wall skirting the edge of the running track which circles the pitch.

When the Turks and Caicos Islands players came out to face their Aruban hosts on a hot and humid May evening, they were stepping out to face an opponent more than seventy places higher in the world rankings than themselves. Despite this huge gulf, they managed to put up an impressive and respectable showing, giving as good as they got. A closely fought contest was decided by a single goal, and sadly for the worst in the world Turks and Caicos, the goal wasn't in their favour. Aruba striker Emile Linkers broke free through the middle with half an hour gone to score with a tidy lobbed finish over the onrushing Turks' keeper Raymondson Azimard.

By that stage, Gavin Glinton had already left the field, succumbing to an early injury and having to be replaced. In his absence, his teammates chased the game late on but failed to muster anything too clear cut. This was in spite of the introduction of record goal scorer Philip Shearer, a few weeks shy of his fortieth birthday, for a final flurry.

Glinton's injury kept him out of the second group match two days later against French Guiana. The result of this match, while being important in the Caribbean Cup of course, would have no bearing on Turks and Caicos' FIFA ranking. French Guiana are not FIFA affiliated, being a part of France rather than an independent nation. In that context, if they were going to get roundly thrashed 6-0 it may as well happen against a team that wouldn't affect their ranking. Had they somehow avoided defeat against French Guiana, as terrific as that would have been, there would surely be a glimmer of lingering frustration that a first positive result in years would still have seen them stuck firmly at the foot of the world rankings. The thorough defeat, however, made that prospect little more than a redundant afterthought.

Again the Turks and Caicos team lost key players during this latest defeat; both midfielder Jack McKnight and goalkeeper Azemard had to be replaced shortly before the opening Guianan goal. Azemard's replacement, a raw untried teenager called Luis Turbyfield, conceded within seconds of coming on late in the first half, before shipping another five in a one-sided second half.

But where there is life there is hope, as they say, and that hope manifested itself in the performances up until that point of their final opponent; the British Virgin Islands. Both teams had suffered six goal hammerings against French Guiana, but while the Turks and Caicos were only narrowly beaten by Aruba, the British Virgin Islands had managed to let in no fewer than seven goals to the group hosts. Both teams were pointless so far, so to speak, and a couple of hours before Aruba and French Guiana would battle it out for group supremacy and qualification for the next round of the Caribbean Cup, the two smallest nations faced off hoping to avoid a whitewash. For the Turks and Caicos Islands, it was a real opportunity to get a positive result and to escape their ranking fate; to finally get that monkey off their back.

It would prove to be a fairly even contest, played out in the oppressive heat of the early evening in Oranjestad. The clash didn't attract much of an audience. The smattering of spectators that were in attendance were dotted about the stands, hiding from the sun under the small main stand's roof. Most of them were little more than curious onlookers; early arrivals for the main event when Aruba played later on.

So it was amid near silence, save for the shouts of encouragement from each team bench, that the players of Turks and Caicos and the British Virgin Islands took to the field. Crucially, Raymondson Azemard was fit enough to take his place in goal and Gavin Glinton was back in the side too. The Turks and Caicos Islands were at full strength, such as it was. Looking for their first win in an international fixture in over six years, they set about their task with purpose. Chances came at both ends of the pitch but it would take a piece of slack defending to cause the breakthrough.

Shortly after half an hour's play, Turks and Caicos' twenty-one year-old striker Marco Fenelus was dangerously gifted the ball in the opposition half and ran into the British Virgin Islands area before firing past the keeper. Having sent his team into a rare lead, he turned sheepishly back towards the halfway line for the restart as though unsure of what to do.

Midway through the second half, it got even better. An attack had broken down but some opportunism saw the ball regained on the left wing and a simple ball across goal, combined with some shoddy defending, left an easy tap in for Stevens Derilien. This time the celebrations were a little more polished. With the dawning realisation that a win really was on the cards, Derilien was mobbed by his jubilant teammates. Those scenes were repeated at the final whistle, albeit with a deal of added exhaustion, when their momentous, significant victory had been declared at long last.

It had been six years in the making, but thanks to the Caribbean Cup and the chance to play the British Virgin Islands, the Turks and Caicos could finally celebrate a win. For the tournament, it meant little more than avoiding finishing last in a mediocre group, but within a wider global perspective it meant so much more to Matthew Green and his band of intrepid players. They had finally raised themselves from the foot of the rankings; no longer the worst in the world.

Worst in the World

Epilogue

Standing on one of Anguilla's tranquil and pristine white sandy beaches, Richard Orlowski's beaming smile provides a clear signal that he is quite content with his lot. On the northern edge of the Leeward Islands, Anguilla is considered a paradise of tropical beauty and seductive calm, even among the rich pickings of the Caribbean.

'It may be a small island, but these guys have the biggest hearts I've ever seen,' said Orlowski, the Polish-born national team coach of Anguilla, referring to his team of amateurs; players who combine international football with careers as construction workers, bankers, teachers and boat builders. 'They leave work early to train and some even risk getting less pay. I feel so much pride when I see them come out on the pitch, how much they juggle in their lives.'[178]

There is pride but there is also pain. Anguilla had become the latest country to join, or in their case to re-join, the exclusive guild of the worst in the world. Bhutan's rise from ranking ignominy as a result of their World Cup qualifying victories over Sri Lanka had propelled them up FIFA's list. Someone had to replace them at the bottom… that team was Anguilla.

'I have a great challenge here,' said Orlowski. 'But I have faith in the players. I know they have potential and I am here to help them achieve something great.' His stewardship could only propel Anguilla in one direction. 'It means nothing to me,' he said of the ranking. 'We've had some bad luck in the past, there's no denying. But now we play in the present. So whoever says that Anguilla don't have a chance, I say to them: "This is football and anything can happen"'[179]

What did happen was that Anguilla lost both legs of their preliminary round play-off in the CONCACAF zone of World Cup qualifying for Russia 2018. Their only remaining ranking points – a lonely and paltry two – dated back to May 2011 and their last positive result was a goalless draw in a friendly match with the US Virgin Islands. Even that limited collection of points would be expunged from the records a few months later. The baton of notoriety, passed from one worst team in the world to the next, had settled in the idyllic islands of the Caribbean once more.

The best hope for Anguilla to escape the clutches of the bottom rung will once again be the Caribbean Cup, as it has been for so many of their close neighbours. It is in these smaller regional tournaments, or in friendlies against carefully selected opposition, that the worst in the world usually find their salvation. The sad reality is that when the smallest, weakest teams play in the biggest and grandest of tournaments, the odds are frequently stacked against them. In World Cup qualifying, as in other continental tournament qualifiers, they are always the lowest seeded teams, always facing superior opposition, and almost always failing.

For European teams that have stumbled their way to the bottom of the world in the past, their prospects have always looked particularly bleak. European qualification always pitched the weakest into groups with teams of vastly greater quality, and never at all set two of the weakest against each other. For San Marino and Andorra, the two Europeans to have served time as the world's worst, that meant the likelihood of a prolonged spell in the club. San Marino in particular remained stuck for years with little hope of escape given their difficult fixture list. Had they the good fortune to have been located in the Caribbean or the South Pacific, rather than in the mountains of Italy's spine, they may well have made good their escape far earlier than they did.

The prospects for Europe's weakest may well be aided in future by the creation of the European Nations' League which will replace some of the less meaningful friendly matches that often clutter the schedule. Away from the primary focus of the top division, those in the lowest tier will finally get the chance to play competitively against their peers. San Marino can take on the likes of Gibraltar, Andorra and the Faroe Islands for supremacy and the chances of years going by without a hint of a win or draw will surely be diminished.

Whoever replaces or joins Anguilla as the worst in the world in the future, if they are to rise from the ashes they will need their players to earn that privilege on the pitch – players who are generally amateur or semi-professional, and who fit training for their national team around their work duties or during extended periods of leave; players who are lured into the world of international football by the pride of representing their country, or that of their ancestors. They play not for riches, but for the love of the game. They play for the glory of their nation even when the prospects of that glory may seem distant and unobtainable. They are the ordinary footballers and ordinary men who get to briefly inhabit a world most of us can only dream about. On a few glorious occasions, they get to rub shoulders with the real elite of the game, competing with them as equals.

Each new team to become worst in the world must find their own Nicky Salapu or Aldo Simoncini; their own Karma Tshering or Jaylee Hodgson. Men who have stared defeat and humiliation in the face time and time again. Men who keep stepping into the firing line to face that prospect once more, regardless of the odds stacked against them, at times in the full glare of repeated mocking and derision. They are the epitome of Theodore Roosevelt's *Man in the Arena*:

It is not the critic who counts; not the man who points out how the strong man stumbles, or where the doer of deeds could have done them better. The credit belongs to the man who is actually in the arena, whose face is marred by dust and sweat and blood; who strives valiantly; who errs, who comes short again and again, because there is no effort without error and shortcoming; but who does actually strive to do the deeds; who knows great enthusiasms, the great devotions; who spends himself in a worthy cause; who at best knows in the end the triumph of high achievement, and who at the worst, if he fails, at least fails while daring greatly, so that his place shall never be with those cold and timid souls who neither know victory nor defeat.

Worst in the World

References

[1] http://bornoffside.net/2014/09/next-goal-wins-interview-nicky-salapu/

[2] http://www.telegraph.co.uk/sport/football/international/3002857/Tonga-routed-as-Socceroos-hit-22.html

[3] http://www.theguardian.com/football/2001/apr/12/newsstory.sport3

[4] http://news.bbc.co.uk/sport1/hi/football/world_cup_2002/1272048.stm

[5] http://www.cbc.ca/sports/soccer/australians-set-world-cup-soccer-scoring-record-1.254320

[6] http://www.telegraph.co.uk/sport/football/international/3003021/Australia-score-31-without-loss-in-record-win.html

[7] http://www.soccertimes.com/wagman/2001/apr12.htm

[8] http://www.telegraph.co.uk/sport/football/international/3003225/FIFA-ruling-which-left-Samoans-singing-the-blues.html

[9] http://www.soccertimes.com/wagman/2001/apr12.htm

[10] http://www.telegraph.co.uk/sport/football/international/3003021/Australia-score-31-without-loss-in-record-win.html

[11] http://news.bbc.co.uk/sport1/hi/football/world_cup_2002/1272048.stm

[12] http://www.telegraph.co.uk/sport/football/international/3003225/FIFA-ruling-which-left-Samoans-singing-the-blues.html

[13] http://www.theguardian.com/sport/blog/2014/jun/03/the-joy-of-six-epic-australian-drubbings

[14] The Other Final (2004) Directed by Johan Kramer [Film]. Netherlands: KesselsKramer

[15] The Other Final (2004) Directed by Johan Kramer [Film]. Netherlands: KesselsKramer

[16] http://news.bbc.co.uk/1/hi/world/americas/4237882.stm

[17] The Other Final (2004) Directed by Johan Kramer [Film]. Netherlands: KesselsKramer

[18] http://www.fifa.com/aboutfifa/footballdevelopment/projects/goalprogramme/status.html

[19] The Other Final (2004) Directed by Johan Kramer [Film]. Netherlands: KesselsKramer

[20] The Other Final (2004) Directed by Johan Kramer [Film]. Netherlands: KesselsKramer

[21] The Other Final (2004) Directed by Johan Kramer [Film]. Netherlands: KesselsKramer

[22] http://www.telegraph.co.uk/travel/destinations/asia/bhutan/730232/Bhutan-Splendid-isolation.html

[23] The Other Final (2004) Directed by Johan Kramer [Film]. Netherlands: KesselsKramer

[24] The Other Final (2004) Directed by Johan Kramer [Film]. Netherlands: KesselsKramer

[25] http://www.theguardian.com/world/2012/dec/01/bhutan-wealth-happiness-counts

[26] http://www.tourism.gov.bt/about-bhutan/the-four-main-pillars

[27] The Other Final (2004) Directed by Johan Kramer [Film]. Netherlands: KesselsKramer

[28] The Other Final (2004) Directed by Johan Kramer [Film]. Netherlands: KesselsKramer

29

http://sportsillustrated.cnn.com/soccer/world/2002/world_cup/news/2002/06/28/bhutan_montserrat_ap/

30

http://sportsillustrated.cnn.com/soccer/world/2002/world_cup/news/2002/06/28/bhutan_montserrat_ap/

31 http://www.raonline.ch/pages/bt/sport/bt_sportfootball03b.html

32 http://www.eaff.com/eanews/news/item468.html

33 www.rsssf.com

34 http://www.eaff.com/eanews/news/item467.html

35 http://mvguam.com/component/content/article/5004-guam-defeats-mongolia-in-eaff-prelims.html#.VQai2NKsXDG

36 http://www.eaff.com/eanews/news/item458.html

37 http://mvguam.com/component/content/article/5004-guam-defeats-mongolia-in-eaff-prelims.html#.VQai2NKsXDG

38 http://www.eaff.com/eanews/news/item468.html

39 http://www.thenational.ae/sport/football/bottom-ranked-fifa-side-bhutan-kick-off-asian-world-cup-qualifying-with-enthusiasm

40 http://www.bbc.co.uk/sport/0/football/31833911

41 http://www.kuenselonline.com/bhutan-participates-in-the-fifa-world-cup-qualifiers-for-the-first-time/

42 http://www.thenational.ae/sport/football/bottom-ranked-fifa-side-bhutan-kick-off-asian-world-cup-qualifying-with-enthusiasm

43 http://www.fifa.com/worldcup/news/y=2015/m=3/news=modest-bhutan-begin-world-cup-adventure-2557343.html

[44] http://www.nytimes.com/2015/03/13/sports/soccer/as-2018-world-cup-qualifying-begins-a-first-for-bhutan.html?&moduleDetail=section-news-1&action=click&contentCollection=Sports&region=Footer&module=MoreInSection&pgtype=article&_r=1

[45] http://www.insideworldfootball.com/world-football/asia/16605-bhutan-and-east-timor-take-giant-killing-strides-in-world-cup-qualifiers

[46] http://www.nytimes.com/2015/03/13/sports/soccer/as-2018-world-cup-qualifying-begins-a-first-for-bhutan.html?&moduleDetail=section-news-1&action=click&contentCollection=Sports&region=Footer&module=MoreInSection&pgtype=article&_r=1

[47] http://www.espnfc.com/world-cup-qualifying-afc/story/2344020/world-cup-begins-in-asia-as-bhutan-win-first-ever-qualifying-game

[48] http://www.theguardian.com/football/blog/2015/mar/16/bhutan-make-history-sri-lanka-world-cup-qualifiers

[49] http://www.npr.org/blogs/thetwo-way/2015/03/17/393552927/bhutan-world-s-last-ranked-soccer-team-advances-in-world-cup

[50] http://www.nytimes.com/2015/03/18/sports/soccer/last-ranked-bhutan-does-it-again-stunning-sri-lanka.html?_r=1

[51] http://www.nytimes.com/2015/03/18/sports/soccer/last-ranked-bhutan-does-it-again-stunning-sri-lanka.html?_r=1

[52] http://www.theguardian.com/football/blog/2015/mar/16/bhutan-make-history-sri-lanka-world-cup-qualifiers

[53] http://www.nytimes.com/2015/03/18/sports/soccer/last-ranked-bhutan-does-it-again-stunning-sri-lanka.html?_r=0

[54] http://uk.reuters.com/article/2008/10/30/soccer-asia-timor-idUKLNE49T08T20081030

[55] http://www.wsc.co.uk/the-archive/921-Asia/5173-emerging-nation

[56] http://asiafoundation.org/in-asia/2008/05/21/from-East Timor-reborn-island-nation-loves-its-soccer-er-football/

[57] http://www.fifa.com/aboutfifa/organisation/homefifa/news/newsid=954330/index.html

[58] http://www.wsc.co.uk/the-archive/921-Asia/5173-emerging-nation

[59] http://asiafoundation.org/in-asia/2008/05/21/from-East Timor-reborn-island-nation-loves-its-soccer-er-football/

[60] http://www.theage.com.au/news/soccer/soccer-pros-main-goal-helping-timor/2007/03/14/1173722558672.html

[61] http://www.wsc.co.uk/the-archive/921-Asia/5173-emerging-nation

[62] http://www.espnfc.com/story/587392

[63] http://www.smh.com.au/news/sport/football/no-league-of-its-own-but-tiny-timor-aims-to-take-on-the-world/2009/05/03/1241289038071.html

[64] http://www.espnfc.com/story/587392

[65] http://www.wsc.co.uk/the-archive/921-Asia/5173-emerging-nation

[66] Next Goal Wins (2014) Directed by Mike Brett and Steve Jamison [Film]. United Kingdom: Icon

[67] http://www.fifa.com/aboutfifa/organisation/president/news/newsid=1365161/index.html

[68] Montague, James (2014). *Thirty-One Nil: The Amazing Story of World Cup Qualification.* United Kingdom. Bloomsbury Publishing

[69] Next Goal Wins (2014) Directed by Mike Brett and Steve Jamison [Film]. United Kingdom: Icon

[70] http://www.fifa.com/world-match-centre/news/newsid/202/829/9/index.html

[71] Next Goal Wins (2014) Directed by Mike Brett and Steve Jamison [Film]. United Kingdom: Icon

[72] Next Goal Wins (2014) Directed by Mike Brett and Steve Jamison [Film]. United Kingdom: Icon

[73] http://www.nytimes.com/2011/11/24/sports/soccer/american-samoa-winless-and-ranked-last-earns-victory-in-a-world-cup-qualifier.html?_r=1

[74] Montague, James (2014). *Thirty-One Nil: The Amazing Story of World Cup Qualification.* United Kingdom. Bloomsbury Publishing

[75] http://www.fifa.com/world-match-centre/news/newsid/202/829/9/index.html

[76] http://espn.go.com/sports/soccer/news/_/id/7323170/american-samoa-dream-team-thomas-rongen-brent-latham-us-soccer

[77] http://www.bbc.co.uk/news/entertainment-arts-27245733

[78] Montague, James (2014). *Thirty-One Nil: The Amazing Story of World Cup Qualification.* United Kingdom. Bloomsbury Publishing

[79] http://www.mirror.co.uk/news/real-life-stories/american-samoa-football-team-transgender-3500369

[80] http://www.fifa.com/world-match-centre/news/newsid/202/829/9/index.html

[81] Next Goal Wins (2014) Directed by Mike Brett and Steve Jamison [Film]. United Kingdom: Icon

[82] http://america.aljazeera.com/articles/2014/4/26/american-samoa-soccer.html

[83] http://www.fifa.com/world-match-centre/news/newsid/202/829/9/index.html

[84] http://bornoffside.net/2014/09/next-goal-wins-interview-nicky-salapu/

[85] Next Goal Wins (2014) Directed by Mike Brett and Steve Jamison [Film]. United Kingdom: Icon

[86] http://www.mirror.co.uk/news/real-life-stories/american-samoa-football-team-transgender-3500369

[87] Next Goal Wins (2014) Directed by Mike Brett and Steve Jamison [Film]. United Kingdom: Icon

[88] Montague, James (2014). *Thirty-One Nil: The Amazing Story of World Cup Qualification*. United Kingdom. Bloomsbury Publishing

[89] http://espn.go.com/sports/soccer/news/_/id/7323170/american-samoa-dream-team-thomas-rongen-brent-latham-us-soccer

[90] http://espn.go.com/sports/soccer/news/_/id/7323170/american-samoa-dream-team-thomas-rongen-brent-latham-us-soccer

[91] Next Goal Wins (2014) Directed by Mike Brett and Steve Jamison [Film]. United Kingdom: Icon

[92] Montague, James (2014). *Thirty-One Nil: The Amazing Story of World Cup Qualification*. United Kingdom. Bloomsbury Publishing

[93] Next Goal Wins (2014) Directed by Mike Brett and Steve Jamison [Film]. United Kingdom: Icon

[94] Montague, James (2014). *Thirty-One Nil: The Amazing Story of World Cup Qualification*. United Kingdom. Bloomsbury Publishing

[95] http://www.out.com/entertainment/sports/2014/06/26/soccer-trans-jayiah-saelua-american-samoa-third-gender-faafafine?page=full

[96] Next Goal Wins (2014) Directed by Mike Brett and Steve Jamison [Film]. United Kingdom: Icon

[97] http://www.nytimes.com/2011/11/26/sports/soccer/jonny-saelua-transgender-player-helps-american-samoa-to-first-international-soccer-win.html?_r=2&

[98] http://america.aljazeera.com/articles/2014/4/26/american-samoa-soccer.html

[99] Montague, James (2014). *Thirty-One Nil: The Amazing Story of World Cup Qualification*. United Kingdom. Bloomsbury Publishing

[100] http://www.fifa.com/worldcup/news/y=2013/m=3/news=drama-and-emotion-oceania-world-cup-path-2050015.html

[101] Next Goal Wins (2014) Directed by Mike Brett and Steve Jamison [Film]. United Kingdom: Icon

[102] Next Goal Wins (2014) Directed by Mike Brett and Steve Jamison [Film]. United Kingdom: Icon

[103] Next Goal Wins (2014) Directed by Mike Brett and Steve Jamison [Film]. United Kingdom: Icon

[104] Next Goal Wins (2014) Directed by Mike Brett and Steve Jamison [Film]. United Kingdom: Icon

[105] Montague, James (2014). *Thirty-One Nil: The Amazing Story of World Cup Qualification*. United Kingdom. Bloomsbury Publishing

[106] Montague, James (2014). *Thirty-One Nil: The Amazing Story of World Cup Qualification*. United Kingdom. Bloomsbury Publishing

[107] http://www.fifa.com/worldcup/news/y=2008/m=3/news=montserrat-mighty-spirit-711579.html

[108] http://www.fifa.com/worldcup/news/y=2008/m=3/news=montserrat-mighty-spirit-711579.html

[109] http://www.fifa.com/worldcup/news/y=2008/m=3/news=montserrat-mighty-spirit-711579.html

[110] Montague, James (2014). *Thirty-One Nil: The Amazing Story of World Cup Qualification*. United Kingdom. Bloomsbury Publishing

[111] Montague, James (2014). *Thirty-One Nil: The Amazing Story of World Cup Qualification*. United Kingdom. Bloomsbury Publishing

[112] Montague, James (2014). *Thirty-One Nil: The Amazing Story of World Cup Qualification*. United Kingdom. Bloomsbury Publishing

[113] Montague, James (2014). *Thirty-One Nil: The Amazing Story of World Cup Qualification*. United Kingdom. Bloomsbury Publishing

[114] http://news.bbc.co.uk/sport1/hi/football/teams/p/port_vale/9504101.stm

[115] http://news.bbc.co.uk/sport1/hi/football/teams/p/port_vale/9504101.stm

[116] http://www.stokesentinel.co.uk/Football-Vale-ace-Griffith-prepares-kick-2014/story-12766788-detail/story.html

[117] http://www.fifa.com/worldcup/news/y=2011/m=6/news=montserrat-date-with-destiny-1451575.html

[118] http://www.bbc.co.uk/sport/0/football/13776058

[119] http://www.fifa.com/worldcup/news/y=2011/m=6/news=montserrat-date-with-destiny-1451575.html

[120] http://www.fifa.com/worldcup/news/y=2011/m=6/news=minnows-take-marks-the-road-rio-1451305.html

[121] Montague, James (2014). *Thirty-One Nil: The Amazing Story of World Cup Qualification*. United Kingdom. Bloomsbury Publishing

[122] Montague, James (2014). *Thirty-One Nil: The Amazing Story of World Cup Qualification*. United Kingdom. Bloomsbury Publishing

[123] http://espn.go.com/sports/soccer/news/_/id/6666022/belize-beats-montserrat-open-qualifying-2014-world-cup

[124] http://www.themontserratreporter.com/what-will-it-be-the-end-of-the-road-to-2014-or-another-chance-forward-for-montserrat/

[125] Montague, James (2014). *Thirty-One Nil: The Amazing Story of World Cup Qualification*. United Kingdom. Bloomsbury Publishing

[126] Montague, James (2014). *Thirty-One Nil: The Amazing Story of World Cup Qualification*. United Kingdom. Bloomsbury Publishing

[127] Montague, James (2014). *Thirty-One Nil: The Amazing Story of World Cup Qualification*. United Kingdom. Bloomsbury Publishing

[128] http://www.themontserratreporter.com/montserrat-represented-at-cfu-football-cup/

[129] http://www.theguardian.com/sport/blog/2012/may/25/joy-of-six-club-country-friendlies

[130] http://www.themontserratreporter.com/montserrat-represented-at-cfu-football-cup/

[131] http://www.theguardian.com/sport/blog/2012/may/25/joy-of-six-club-country-friendlies

[132] http://www.fourfourtwo.com/features/whats-it-play-san-marino-players-tell-fft-theres-nothing-lose

[133] http://www.fifa.com/worldcup/news/y=2013/m=3/news=mazza-results-are-not-priority-2029351.html

[134] http://www.uefa.com/uefaeuro/qualifiers/news/newsid=2055206.html

[135] http://www.dailymail.co.uk/sport/football/article-2467211/San-Marino-boss-Giampaolo-Mazza-resigns-earning-just-point-15-years.html

[136] http://www.fifa.com/worldcup/news/y=2013/m=3/news=mazza-results-are-not-priority-2029351.html

[137] Montague, James (2014). *Thirty-One Nil: The Amazing Story of World Cup Qualification*. United Kingdom. Bloomsbury Publishing

[138] http://www.fifa.com/worldcup/news/y=2013/m=3/news=mazza-results-are-not-priority-2029351.html

[139] http://sports.ndtv.com/football/news/16491-germany-hammers-san-marino-13-0

[140] Montague, James (2014). *Thirty-One Nil: The Amazing Story of World Cup Qualification*. United Kingdom. Bloomsbury Publishing

[141] Montague, James (2014). *Thirty-One Nil: The Amazing Story of World Cup Qualification*. United Kingdom. Bloomsbury Publishing

[142] http://www.fifa.com/worldcup/news/y=2013/m=3/news=mazza-results-are-not-priority-2029351.html

[143] http://www.telegraph.co.uk/sport/football/teams/england/9602709/England-v-San-Marino-All-we-are-saying-is-give-us-a-goal...-the-cry-from-worlds-worst-team-ahead-of-Wembley-clash.html

[144] http://www.dailymail.co.uk/sport/football/article-2296836/Remember-San-Marino-1993-What-happened-Englands-World-Cup-humiliation-.html

[145] http://www.mirror.co.uk/sport/football/news/england-exclusive-davide-gualtieri-interview-1371253

[146] http://www.mirror.co.uk/sport/football/news/england-exclusive-davide-gualtieri-interview-1371253

[147] http://www.mirror.co.uk/sport/football/news/england-exclusive-davide-gualtieri-interview-1371253

[148] http://www.dailymail.co.uk/sport/football/article-2296836/Remember-San-Marino-1993-What-happened-Englands-World-Cup-humiliation-.html

[149] http://www.mirror.co.uk/sport/football/news/england-exclusive-davide-gualtieri-interview-1371253

[150] http://www.telegraph.co.uk/sport/football/teams/england/9602709/England-v-San-Marino-All-we-are-saying-is-give-us-a-goal...-the-cry-from-worlds-worst-team-ahead-of-Wembley-clash.html

[151] http://www.bbc.co.uk/sport/0/football/29530004

[152] http://www.bbc.co.uk/sport/0/football/29530004

[153] http://www.mirror.co.uk/sport/football/news/england-v-san-marino-meet-1373512

[154] http://www.uefa.com/uefaeuro/qualifiers/news/newsid=2055206.html

[155] http://www.theguardian.com/football/blog/2014/oct/08/san-marino-fifa-whipping-boys

[156] http://www.uefa.com/uefaeuro/qualifiers/news/newsid=2055206.html

[157] http://www1.skysports.com/football/news/11095/9509352/european-qualifiers-san-marino-manager-pierangelo-manzaroli-looks-to-limit-damage

[158] http://www.bbc.co.uk/sport/0/football/29530004

[159] http://www.mirror.co.uk/sport/football/news/england-vs-san-marino-aldo-4404172

[160] http://www.bbc.co.uk/sport/0/football/29530004

[161] https://www.vice.com/en_uk/read/the-certainty-of-defeat-an-interview-with-the-goalkeeper-of-the-worlds-worst-national-team-876

[162] http://www.thesportbible.com/articles/thesportbible-interviews-san-marino-goalkeeper-aldo-simoncini

[163] https://www.vice.com/en_uk/read/the-certainty-of-defeat-an-interview-with-the-goalkeeper-of-the-worlds-worst-national-team-876

[164] https://www.vice.com/en_uk/read/the-certainty-of-defeat-an-interview-with-the-goalkeeper-of-the-worlds-worst-national-team-876

[165] http://www.talkingbaws.com/2014/12/03/zlatan-ibrahimovic-shows-his-caring-side-to-tragic-san-marino-keeper/

[166] http://www.talkingbaws.com/2014/12/03/zlatan-ibrahimovic-shows-his-caring-side-to-tragic-san-marino-keeper/

167

http://www.uefa.com/uefaeuro/qualifiers/season=2016/matches/round=200044
6/match=2013903/postmatch/quotes/

168

http://www.uefa.com/uefaeuro/qualifiers/season=2016/matches/round=200044
6/match=2013903/postmatch/quotes/

169

http://edition.cnn.com/2011/SPORT/football/09/13/football.us.virgin.islands/

[170] http://www.planetworldcup.com/CUPS/2006/tci_story.html

[171] http://www.bloomberg.com/news/articles/2013-10-21/fifa-grants-seen-
wasted-as-blatter-roadshow-arrives-in-caribbean

[172] http://www.planetworldcup.com/CUPS/2006/tci_story.html

[173] http://www.theguardian.com/football/2008/jun/07/1

[174] http://www.bbc.co.uk/sport/0/football/24549624

[175] http://www.theguardian.com/football/2008/jun/07/1

[176] http://www.theguardian.com/football/2008/jun/07/1

[177] http://www.bbc.co.uk/sport/0/football/24549624

[178] http://www.fifa.com/worldcup/news/y=2015/m=3/news=anguilla-out-on-
the-edge-2568973.html

[179] http://www.fifa.com/worldcup/news/y=2015/m=3/news=anguilla-out-on-
the-edge-2568973.html

Other Books from Bennion Kearny

José Mourinho: The Rise of the Translator by Ciaran Kelly

From Porto to Chelsea, and Inter to Real Madrid – the Mourinho story is as intriguing as the man himself. Now, a new challenge awaits at Stamford Bridge. Covering the Mourinho story to October 2013 and featuring numerous exclusive interviews with figures not synonymous with the traditional Mourinho narrative.

"Enlightening interviews with those who really know José Mourinho" – Simon Kuper, Financial Times.

"Superb read from a terrific writer" – Ger McCarthy, Irish Examiner

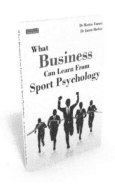

What Business Can Learn From Sport Psychology: Ten Lessons for Peak Professional Performance by Dr Martin Turner & Dr Jamie Barker

It goes without saying that business performance has many parallels with sporting performance. But did you realize that the scientific principles of sport psychology, used by elite athletes the world over, are being used by some of the most successful business professionals? Performance - in any context - is about utilizing and deploying every possible resource to fulfil your potential.

With this book you will develop the most important weapon you need to succeed in business: your mental approach to performance. This book reveals the secrets of the winning mind by exploring the strategies and techniques used by the most successful athletes and professionals on the planet.

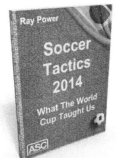

Soccer Tactics 2014: What The World Cup taught Us by Ray Power

Soccer Tactics 2014 analyses the intricacies of modern international systems, through the lens of matches in Brazil. Covering formations, game plans, key playing positions, and individuals who bring football tactics to life - the book offers analysis and insights for soccer coaches, football players, and fans the world over.

Whether it is Tiki-Taka, counter-attacking, or David defending heroically to defeat Goliath - this book sheds light on where football tactics currently stand… and where they are going.

Graduation: Life Lessons of a Professional Footballer by Richard Lee

The 2010/11 season will go down as a memorable one for Goalkeeper Richard Lee. Cup wins, penalty saves, hypnotherapy and injury would follow, but these things only tell a small part of the tale. Filled with anecdotes, insights, humour and honesty - Graduation uncovers Richard's campaign to take back the number one spot, save a lot of penalties, and overcome new challenges. What we see is a transformation - beautifully encapsulated in this extraordinary season.

The Way Forward: Solutions to England's Football Failings by Matthew Whitehouse

English football is in a state of crisis. It has been almost 50 years since England made the final of a major championship and the national sides, at all levels, continue to disappoint and underperform. Yet no-one appears to know how to improve the situation. In The Way Forward, football coach Matthew Whitehouse examines the causes of English football's decline and offers a number of areas where change and improvement need to be implemented immediately. With a keen focus and passion for youth development and improved coaching he explains that no single fix can overcome current difficulties and that a multi-pronged strategy is needed. If we wish to improve the standards of players in England then we must address the issues in schools, the grassroots, and academies, as well as looking at the constraints of the Premier League and English FA.

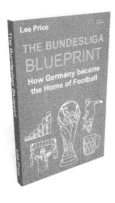

The Bundesliga Blueprint: How Germany became the Home of Football by Lee Price

German Football is on a roll: winners of the 2014 World Cup, club sides leading the way in Europe, a production line of superb talent coming through the system. Yet, fifteen years ago, at Euro 2000 – it was all so different. Germany suffered one of their most humiliating tournament exits as dismal performances saw them finish bottom of their group with just one point… Immediately, the German FA set about fixing things. And rather than fudging matters, they introduced a raft of major changes designed to return German football to it sporting pinnacle in just 10 years.

In this entertaining, fascinating, and superbly-researched book, sportswriter Lee Price explores German football's 10-year plan. A plan that forced clubs to invest in youth, limit the number of foreign players in teams, build success without debt, and much more. *The Bundesliga Blueprint* details how German fans part-own and shape their clubs, how football is affordable, and the value of beer and a good sausage on match days. The book includes interviews from Michael Ballack, Jen Nowotny and Christoph Kramer, and the movers-and-shakers behind Germany's leading clubs including Schalke, Dortmund, and Paderborn. There is no doubt that German football is the envy of many nations. There is no doubt that, thanks to them, lessons should be learned by everyone else.

Universality | The Blueprint for Soccer's New Era: How Germany and Pep Guardiola are showing us the Future Football Game by Matthew Whitehouse

The game of soccer is constantly in flux; new ideas, philosophies and tactics mould the present and shape the future. In this book, Matthew Whitehouse – acclaimed author of The Way Forward: Solutions to England's Football Failings - looks in-depth at the past decade of the game, taking the reader on a journey into football's evolution. Examining the key changes that have occurred since the turn of the century, right up to the present, the book looks at the evolution of tactics, coaching, and position-specific play. They have led us to this moment: to the rise of universality. Universality | The Blueprint For Soccer's New Era is a voyage into football, as well as a lesson for coaches, players and fans who seek to know and anticipate where the game of the future is heading.

See all our Football Books: **www.BennionKearny.com/soccer**

Lightning Source UK Ltd.
Milton Keynes UK
UKOW06f1527190216

268732UK00008B/217/P